WINDOWS
OF THE
SOUL

WINDOWS OF THE SOUL

A Look at Dreams and Their Meanings

Paul Meier, M.D.
Robert L. Wise, Ph.D.

A
JANET
THOMA
BOOK

THOMAS NELSON PUBLISHERS
Nashville • Atlanta • London • Vancouver

Published in Nashville, Tennessee, by Thomas Nelson, Inc., Publishers, and distributed in Canada by Word Communications, Ltd., Richmond, British Columbia.

Unless otherwise noted, Scripture references are from THE NEW KING JAMES VERSION. Copyright © 1979, 1980, 1982, 1990, Thomas Nelson, Inc., Publishers.

Scripture quotations noted RSV are from the REVISED STANDARD VERSION of the Bible. Copyright © 1946, 1952, 1971, 1973 by the Division of Christian Education of the National Council of the Churches of Christ in the U.S.A. Used by permission.

Anecdotes and case histories described in this volume are composites drawn from actual cases. Details have been changed to protect the identities of the persons involved.

Library of Congress Cataloging-in-Publication Data

Meier, Paul D.
    Windows of the soul : a psychiatrist and a minister look at dreams and their meanings / Paul Meier and Robert Wise.
        p.   cm.
    Includes bibliographical references.
    ISBN 0-7852-7866-4
    1. Dreams.   2. Dream interpretation.   3. Spiritual life.   I. Wise, Robert L.
II. Title.
BF1091.M45   1995
154.6'3—dc20   95-6250
                                                                              CIP

Printed in the United States of America.

1 2 3 4 5 6 — 01 00 99 98 97 96 95

To Ayesha Rebekah and Brooke Elise Wise—
two dreams come true.

CONTENTS

ACKNOWLEDGMENTS

Without the help and pastoral care of our friends in the community of Pecos, New Mexico, this book would not have been possible. Robert Wise remains particularly indebted to Abbot David Gaerats, his spiritual director, for teaching and leading him on the path of insight and growth through dream work.

Our deepest appreciation to Robert and Retha Bierschank for their tireless work in typing, revising, and proofing the copy. We are also grateful to Janet Thoma, as always, for her excellent editorial expertise.

Chapter 1

DREAM
TRAILS

Starting a Journey

How much there is in the Bible about dreams! There are, I think, some sixteen chapters in the Old Testament and four or five in the New in which dreams are mentioned; and there are many other passages scattered throughout the book which refer to visions. If we believe in the Bible, we must accept the fact that, in the old days, God and his angels came to humans in their sleep and made themselves known in dreams.

ABRAHAM LINCOLN

The waves of the Galilee splashed against the Tiberius landing as Paul Meier and Robert Wise sat in a quaint local café eating supper, talking after completing a day of touring the surrounding villages of the ancient sea. During the afternoon they had walked through the remains of the biblical town of Capernaum and stood on the hillside where the Beatitudes were delivered. At the end of the day they always discussed the research on the current book they were completing. The warm breeze from the lake made them feel drowsy. They were tired.

"Ought to make for great sleeping," Robert remarked. "Should be good dreams tonight."

"If I can remember them," Paul answered with a laugh. "Robert, you've studied dreams for years. What started your interest in dreams?"

For several moments Robert stared at the seagulls circling the wooden dock. No reminiscences were needed to answer that question! The response always came immediately, but words took longer. Sometimes he still felt very uncomfortable sharing the experience. Paul was a good friend and a nationally known psychiatrist, but Robert was still reluctant to talk about one of the most personal dimensions of his life.

Robert's earliest recollections began with *the* dream. In many respects this one dream was almost his first memory. The same story returned again and again throughout his entire childhood and adolescent years. For many years he had thought the dream was an actual experience, not a reverie. The images of the three-year-old lost child are always there ready for instant replay.

In the dream, he is playing in and around rows of tall cotton plants. The hot summer wind blows through the stalks, shaking the fluffy white bolls waiting to be picked. He sees a group of workers being loaded into the back of a truck down at the far end of the field.

Instantly he knows his mother is being loaded into the truck with the workers! The dreamscape is filled with fear. He's going to be left if he can't get to the pickup! He runs as hard as his small legs will carry him, but he can't move fast enough. A straggly root grabs his ankle, sending him sprawling into the green stalks. Panic sweeps over him. He is about to drown in a flood of emotion.

The truck roars to life, and the tailgate slams shut. Nothing can stop the truck. Fear erupts in a volcano of screams and cries, but

Robert can't do anything. The truck lumbers away, sending dirt flying in every direction. His mother disappears in a cloud of dust. He is left in the field, alone, terrified, tears running down his cheeks. *Abandoned.*

Robert's thoughts were interrupted by Paul. "Your dreams seem to give you extra insight many pastors don't have."

Robert nodded mechanically, thinking about how this single dream had shaped his life. The mystery of his separation from his original parents had shrouded and encased his life in an enigma. He wasn't sure what was memory, dream, hope, or projection. His dream certainly expressed a longing to find something, someone, someplace that had been ripped out of his life long ago.

"I know you've helped a lot of people," Paul said. "Have you ever thought about writing a book on the subject?"

"Strange you should ask," Robert answered. "I have a file of dreams from people I've worked with over the years, as well as my own dream journals extending over more than a decade. Many of the breakthroughs I've seen in spiritual direction came from working with powerful dreams. Some wild episodes are tucked away in there! Yes, I've often thought the public could profit from many of the insights I've discovered through the years."

"Dreams are a very important part of my life," Paul said thoughtfully. "Many sections in my books came from being awakened in the night with new key insights. And I'm really fascinated by the importance dreams have for my own patients. It's amazing what we can learn about people by hearing just one dream.

"Let me tell you a really wild story." Paul's eyes twinkled; he smiled broadly. "On November 15, 1989, I was driving to my parents' home after finishing a day of seeing patients in a Dallas hospital. As always, I was listening to the Bible on cassette tapes, which allows me to hear the entire Bible several times a year. The words were ringing in my ears: 'You laid affliction on our backs. You have caused men to ride over our heads; we went through fire and through water; but You brought us out to rich fulfillment.'"[1]

Paul's grin vanished. "As I made a left turn I realized I was in the path of an oncoming car. Before I could react, the vehicle hit me in the right side at a speed of over fifty miles an hour. My car folded like an accordion, flipped into the air, and spun around above the ground. People in other cars looked as if they were literally 'riding over my head.' Before I even had time to feel anything, the thought raced through my mind, *This is what God has in store for me at this moment in my life.* Suddenly my ears were filled with the crashing noise of the roof of the car smashing into the pavement."

"You could have been killed!" Robert exclaimed. "You must have been showered with broken glass. Any bones broken?"

Paul's schoolboy grin returned. "At that moment I didn't know that the night before my mother-in-law had been awakened in the night by a deeply disturbing dream. The nightmare gave Eva immediate concern for the well-being of her children and she began praying fervently that God would protect them and their mates each day. Eva had been impressed with the words from Psalm 91, 'He who dwells in the secret place of the Most High shall abide under the shadow of the Almighty. . . . He shall deliver you from the snare of the fowler and from the perilous pestilence.'[2] My mother-in-law had prayed this promise for me because of a dream, and now I was about to reap the benefits of God's constant care. A dream had set the stage for intercessory prayer that probably saved my life."

"Don't stop now," Robert urged. "What happened?"

"When my car landed upside down, the seat belt kept me suspended barely one inch from the pavement below me. 'Affliction' was laid on my back." Paul rolled his eyes. "Steam was spewing out of the hood, and instantly I knew the car could explode in flames. I unfastened the seat belt and crawled out a smashed window, taking the cassette recorder with me. Both cars were totaled, yet neither I nor the driver of the other car had a scratch! Dazed by the collision,

I still remained calm and steady. The heavenly Father had brought me 'through fire and through water to rich fulfillment.'"

"What an incredible story, Paul! Amazing!" Robert said.

"By the time the policeman arrived, the ambulance was driving off. Assuming I was a witness, the officer asked, 'Are they already carrying the dead away?' When he discovered I was the driver, the policeman nearly went into shock!"

"What happened next?" Robert asked.

Paul shrugged. "Oh, I would have been stranded but a couple of ladies who stopped recognized me from my television shows and offered me a ride home. The delay caused by the wreck was actually quite minimal."

Robert chuckled. "Chauffeured home like a celebrity!"

Paul again became serious. "After such an exhausting day, I needed to turn in early. To my amazement the wild escapades of the day were followed by another adventure in the night. I dreamed I was to listen to the rest of the Psalms on the tape until one particular passage truly spoke to me. The next morning I immediately turned on the tape machine. I paid rapt attention and found the message, 'Teach us to number our days, that we may gain a heart of wisdom.'[3] After my accident, my mother-in-law's dream, my dream, and hearing that message, I decided to develop a new habit. Each morning I would awake thanking God for *that day*. I was compelled to rededicate my life in a new way. I would live for Him *one day at a time!*"

Paul didn't have to say anything more. Robert knew what overwhelming moments follow such insights. And he knew that if they both put their experiences on paper, he and Paul could help many people.

Robert Wise's dream work actually began during a sabbatical in Pecos, New Mexico, at the Benedictine Abbey, where he had gone to study the meaning of the soul. His college transcripts were filled with work on the mind and emotions, but no one seemed to know much about studying the soul. These believers had collected centuries of Christian thought and experience on the recovery of the soul through prayer and worship. The Benedictines discovered the importance of dreams for the first Christians. Their concern and ministry started Robert in the work of understanding the subject.

"I spent endless frustrating hours trying to get hold of the meaning of my dreams," Robert recalled. "I felt like a moron trying to learn algebra. Suddenly one afternoon the rock over the cave in my mind moved, and the meaning of the dream from the previous night opened before me.

"In that dream I was running around telling people what to do. I was completely preoccupied with directing what everyone in the monastic community should be doing. Then the dream shifted, and I appeared as an older man wearing a Humphrey Bogart forties-style hat and a *Casablanca* trenchcoat. My beard was white, and I seemed much older by the time the dream was completed.

"The longer I looked at my dream, the less I seemed to understand. My frustration mounted, and I prayed for guidance. Suddenly the principles the Benedictines had taught me clicked. The 'Robert' in the dream was actually representative of my very rational controlling side. I was trying to get everything under control instead of allowing the more intuitive part of my mind to have freedom. I realized I needed to quit acting like a busybody and start functioning like a detective—like soft-hearted Rick in the classic film *Casablanca* saying, 'Play it again, Sam.' If I just let the answers 'come up,' they would. I realized I could become a much wiser person by listening to the intuitive side of my personality."

Insight came rushing in with profound satisfaction. Robert was excited! He had found the way to his dream world! Since that day his life has been profoundly enriched and his personality better integrated because of the insight from his dreams.

"You're right," he told Paul. "We obviously have been deeply touched by the power of dreaming. We have a story to tell about how a psychiatrist and a minister have both been helped by and can help people recover the healing power of dreams."

Paul extended his hand. "Well, the night's before us. What better time to start a book on dreams?"

On that evening by the Sea of Galilee their journey began. The dream trails have been exciting to travel. Robert and Paul invite you to join them now. In the following pages they share the story of their trek across the dreamland terrain of mind and soul. They want you to accompany them in an incredible adventure toward wholeness and new discoveries about yourself that can set you free from the shackles of the past.

What Can You Expect?

What will you find if you look at dreams? What's out there waiting for discovery in your dreamscapes? Endless surprising insights! You have a private movie theater, your own unique television channel that plays a first-run premier production every night. You just need to learn how to tune in and read between the lines.

You dream every night. Everyone does. Whether or not you're fully in touch with the experience, the best scientific research assures us if we *don't* dream we quickly lose stability. Positively, your dreams are attempting to give you vital information. This book will show you how to tune in and get the message.

Of the greatest significance of all, your heavenly Father may just be trying to get in touch with you through these night calls. Both Robert Wise, a minister, and Paul Meier, a psychiatrist with a degree in theology, know the spiritual value of dreams.

Do you have reservations? Look at the Bible.

Both the Old and New Testaments contain numerous dream stories. God communicated direction and warnings to His chosen people through their dreams.

Many literary classics are based on dream experiences. Some of the most interesting stories ever written were either the product of dreams or about dreaming. Robert Louis Stevenson's classic, *Dr. Jekyll and Mr. Hyde,* came from Stevenson's own dream about his own dual nature. His book was actually about the hidden shadow side we all have. *Frankenstein* was written by Mary Shelley after dreaming the story. While the book spawned a rash of mere horror stories, Shelley was actually encountering her own hidden capacity to do monstrous things. The inner beast needed love to be transformed. Unfortunately, Hollywood didn't understand the real message embodied in Shelley's metaphor monster. Of course, *Alice in Wonderland* was a little girl's dream, as was *The Wizard of Oz.* Each story had a common denominator; a hidden, profound meaning often eludes the casual reader. The real secret lies in the symbolic meaning of the dream.

Every morning, people sit down to a cup of coffee and share the previous night's dream adventures. People often have amazing stories of how their lives were changed by their dreams.

Face the facts! *Everyone dreams every night!*

The real question is whether you are in touch with the meaning of these nighttime narratives. We have good news for you. The time has come to understand more fully what God is telling you in your sleep. The messages will surprise and delight you.

Robert Wise knows the capacity of dreams to affect the course of one's life. His own recurring childhood dream of being abandoned in a field became a major motivating force in searching for his origins and seeking his original family. The quest took forty years to complete, but the need for wholeness shaped everything he did along the way. Trying to unravel the mystery of the dream, whether or not it was actually the fragments of a personal experience, sent him to Europe and to Israel, searching both historical records and studying dream work. Later in the book Robert will share more details of this amazing, many-colored dream story.

In retrospect, Robert came to see how the Holy Spirit uses dreams not only for communication and for personal edification and growth, but also to guide our lives through these dream trails. Robert's childhood recurring dream was part of a much larger plan to bring his personal fulfillment.

Your Personal Road Map

In this book, Robert Wise and Paul Meier are going to help you learn how to understand and discover the meaning of your dreams. You'll learn what a dream actually is, and you'll come to understand the nature of the strange and difficult symbolic language of the unconscious. The time-tested approach to dissecting the story line of a dream will allow you to understand your dreams as well as to develop new perspectives on your personality.

In the process of doing dream work, you'll be able to get in touch with areas of your life that need attention and nurture. Each insight will help you become a more integrated and whole person.

You will discover the important place dreams have in the Scriptures and how biblical people received divine messages through their dreams. The historical testimony of the last twenty centuries bears ample witness that the same system of communication continues to this very hour. Dreams can be a divinely appointed link in our connection with Providence.

As your discernment develops, so will your capacity to understand yourself and others. Few pursuits are as satisfying as dream work. This is one time you get ready by turning the lights *out* and closing your eyes. Here we go!

Sweet dreams.

Chapter 2

OPENING THE
SECRETS OF
THE NIGHT

Deciphering the Dream

*I dreamed I had a child, and even in the dream I
saw it was my life, and it was an idiot, and I ran
away. But it always crept onto my lap again,
clutched at my clothes. Until I thought, if I could
kiss it, whatever in it was my own, perhaps I could
sleep. And I bent to its broken face, and it was
horrible . . . but I kissed it. I think one must
finally take one's life in one's arms. . . .*
            ARTHUR MILLER, *AFTER THE FALL*

In 1991, Dr. Paul Meier found himself in the middle of
an amazing dream that precipitated a remarkable series
of events. Like the character facing disillusionment in Arthur
Miller's play, cited above, Paul was about to take a fall. In dealing
with his own self-revelations during this period he suddenly found
himself having to confront the meaning of his own weakness.

Paul remembers, "I was unaware trouble was brewing with my

youngest daughter. The situation reached a crisis point when Elizabeth left home for a short period. My wife Jan and I were shocked.

"Fortunately, Elizabeth turned to a Christian counselor for help. Without my knowledge she began trying to unpack her emotional baggage. She had become depressed because I was far too critical. Finally the counselor called, asking Jan and me to meet for a family session at 9:00 A.M. on a Saturday morning.

"I readily and enthusiastically agreed, then hung up. But in truth I had lied! The whole idea was very irritating, humiliating, and embarrassing for me. After all, I am a psychiatrist! What could some half-baked counselor tell me about what I might be contributing to my daughter's depression? After all, I had written books on how to raise children correctly! I knew quite well the whole dynamic of what was going to happen come Saturday morning. Frankly, I didn't want to go at all. It's much easier to tell other parents what *they* are doing wrong!

"Friday night I went to bed with the next day's confrontation on my mind. While I wouldn't have admitted it, I was getting my strategy lined up for the next morning's counseling session. Before dawn broke, my sleep was invaded by a horrible dream. There was no question that God Himself was confronting me. With great intensity, the heavenly Father brought before my mind a personalized passage of Scripture I had memorized years before:

> Why do you look at the speck in your [daughter's] eye, but do not consider the plank in your own eye? Or how can you say to your [daughter], 'Let me remove the speck from your eye'; and look, a plank is in your own eye? Hypocrite! First remove the plank from your own eye, and then you will see clearly to remove the speck from your [daughter's] eye.[1]

"I awoke in deep distress. The impact of the words left me weeping. For the first time I saw the real possibility that I had played a major part in my daughter's depression. I had ignored an important truth about myself. Immediately I began praying about my hypocrisy until I could go back to sleep.

"The next morning I was too embarrassed to discuss the dream. Jan and I silently left for the meeting with the Christian counselor. The young man was obviously competent, sincere, and ready to face the issues head-on. Without a great deal of fanfare, the counselor suggested that we might get at the issues quickly by considering a passage of Scripture that would put my daughter's feelings into context. To my surprise he opened a Bible and began reading, 'Why do you look at the speck in your brother's eye, but do not consider the plank in your own?'

"I couldn't help myself. I began weeping aloud. He stopped reading and everyone looked at me in astonishment. In simple, straightforward terms, I told them the story of my dream.

"By the time I finished, we were all overwhelmed. Needless to say, the counseling session was a great success. With all due respect to the young man, God had already set things in motion by calling me in the night."

In Paul's dream, the Scriptures were used to convey both a literal and a symbolic meaning. The direct message was clear enough, but Paul also recognized an inner meaning. Our contemporary way of talking about the "speck in the eye" is called *projection*. We criticize in others what we are most uncomfortable with in ourselves. Paul needed to face some personal issues. Insight completely changed his response to the family situation.

How did Paul recognize the message in his dream? Because he understood dreams, Paul was able to find significant insight into his experience. We can have the same insight into dream structure.

Sooner or later we all have our own unique collision with reality and need all the help possible to pick up our lives and breathe meaning back into the past. Because dreams can help us accomplish this, as Paul's dream did, we all need to know what is happening behind the scenes of these nightly scenarios.

Finding a dream's meaning was also helpful to Linda, who began to discuss a disturbing recurring dream soon after she first came in for counseling. At the time Linda was facing a divorce.

In the dream George, a distant friend, appears in front of Linda's house intending to kill both of them. She looks out to discover George's car parked in front of her house. Linda runs out and opens the car door. To her astonishment, George tumbles out. Desperately she gives CPR but can't bring George back to life. Linda becomes aware of neighbors standing around watching and laughing at her. They keep pointing and admonishing that the entire situation is her fault. Linda awakes feeling consternation and mystification.

Start Paying Attention

Our sleep is filled with important secrets that will help us understand the handwriting of our lost memories. In order to understand Linda's dream, we need more information on the meaning of her dream components. We must look at this subject from many diverse angles; it's like walking around a mountain and looking at the hill from many different sides. We're not after an answer in an algebra problem as much as we are developing a new perception of the meaning of the dream experience.

You may not yet be convinced that everyone dreams every night. The issue isn't frequency but attention to the fact. Often people are so out of touch with themselves they have no sense of their dreams.

When Linda tuned in, she discovered her recurring dream was symptomatic of a specific unresolved problem. Many people report the same dream popping up for years, just as Robert Wise repeatedly dreamed of seeing his mother being loaded into the pickup in that field. Recurring dreams or variations thereof keep coming back until the buried issue is unearthed and faced.

In Ann Faraday's book *The Dream Game,* researchers broadly categorize dreamers as either "recallers" or "nonrecallers."[2] The difference seems to lie more in interest and attentiveness than in any innate capacity. Engineers are less in tune than artists; men are less attuned than women. However, once people *want* to tune in, they become aware of what is happening in their slumbers.

We dream in cycles. The first period of dreaming begins after about ninety minutes of sleep and lasts from five to ten minutes. As the cycles recur in ninety-minute segments, the dreams get longer. The last cycle may last as long as forty minutes, and generally it produces the most significant dream.

Researchers chart these periods by observing rapid eye movements (REMs). Extended periods of REMs disprove the idea that dreams last only a few seconds. In fact, one method of getting in touch with dreams is to be wakened during the active cycle until we become aware of our inner journey.[3]

Dreams and sleep follow a predictable pattern. We begin by slipping into a deep, hypnoticlike trance. Next we drop into a complete state of suspended awareness and lose all consciousness. As the cycle swings upward, the dream begins to emerge gradually becoming structured and significant. As sleep progresses, the dream may even become more real than waking experiences.

During the REM periods of activity, the dream accomplishes significant work. How important is this work? When people are not allowed to dream, eventually they will become severely mentally disturbed, depressed, or even psychotic.

What Is a Dream?

A scientific description of a dream becomes increasingly complex the longer we attempt an exact definition. The easiest answer is, "What you remember from your sleep." However, we need something more substantial.

Lawrence Kubie's article on "Blocks to Creativity" in *International Science and Technology* described the mind as a magnificent computer that never ceases to operate but needs downtime to recuperate. While rational thinking is the primary activity, the secondary unobserved function creates intuitive wisdom. During sleep, the unconscious mind is, in effect, shuffling papers, filing, and cataloging old events while processing the implications of our experience. Dreams are the wisdom, insight, and messages from the unconscious realm seeking expression in our full awareness. Behind the dream is a drive toward wholeness and completeness. Kubie's description suggests dreams can be defined as the mind's inner method of unlocking potential.[4]

Seen from another angle, dreams are often a substitute for actual experience. We can live through what we haven't yet encountered as event. Revisiting the implications of previous events or wrestling with what might lie ahead saves us from disasters we would otherwise experience.

Here's a concrete way to describe these abstract functions. Let us introduce you to an inner friend. Think of your mind as being filled with little people who do the computer work required for thinking. You have your own personal late-night movie producer living upstairs in your thought life. Even Hollywood couldn't create as sophisticated, creative, imaginative, and insightful a cinematographer as is the dream processor within you. Meet your moviemaker.

Your benefactor wants you to be in touch with the real world in the same way highly sensitive artists are profoundly aware of the meaning of human experience. This highly intelligent comrade knows what every true writer, artist, and playwright thrives on. The most significant way to communicate insight is not through abstract discussion but by embodiment in a powerful story. The dreamer within is relaying messages through extraordinary stories. Often these tales of the heart are cast in very absurd terms and strange convolutions. But how better could your alter ego get your attention?

Try it from this angle: See yourself in the Louvre standing before a masterpiece by van Gogh or Cezanne. You study the use of color, technique, and light to get the real message of the picture. You try to look through the painter's eyes. The better you understand the artist's meaning, the more profound is your insight into the world around you. What happens to you when you see great movies like *Shadowlands, Chariots of Fire,* or *Schindler's List?* You are impacted with profound awareness and a new perspective you didn't have before.

Your dream-producing inner companion is working toward the same goal. A dream is a story filled with hidden meaning and a definite moral that can profoundly help in your life pilgrimage toward wholeness.

Linda and Paul's dreams were analogous to sitting through movie versions portraying their personal problems. Each story ended with a solution for their daily dilemmas. The answers were in the hidden meaning of the dream cinema.

Perhaps you're saying, "Wait a minute. I never did understand modern art or plays like Arthur Miller's *After the Fall.* You're going to have to throw me more rope if you're going to pull me ashore." Sure. We all need help finding our way into the symbolic world where truth is embodied in objects and stories.

Let's Go to the Movies

Modern psychoanalytic thinkers offer important instruction in the art of interpretation of dreams. Their exploration of how the deep mind formulates its messages and sends them up during our sleep is instructive. We don't have to buy all of their theories to appropriate helpful insights. Let's start with Sigmund Freud, the first medical person to take the effects of dreams seriously.

Freud found that the unconscious mind deals with deep disturbing urges and feelings by encasing them in symbolic form. The dream often represents wish fulfillment of hidden desires. Freud postulated dreams use symbols because of a reluctance to face the facts about our own tendencies.

Freud believed dreams primarily disguise hidden sexual urges. We can't understand the story line because we are actually afraid to fess up. He thought the fundamental issue is almost always sexual. While the academic world was initially enthralled with the idea of a hidden sexual meaning, in time academia became disenchanted with Freud's obsession with sexual conflict, finally recognizing that Freud's extensive theories were actually based on limited experience with a very small number of patients. In his entire career, Freud fully psychoanalyzed fewer than a half-dozen people, most of whom were victims of Victorian repression rather than representatives of universal experience.

Dr. Carl G. Jung, the Swiss psychoanalyst, built on Freud's foundation but took a radically different path. He analyzed thousands of dreams over decades from a wide range of clients. Jung's studies were vast and comprehensive. He quickly saw that dream symbols aren't trying to camouflage content but instead are trying to accomplish exactly the opposite. Dream symbols give us the most comprehensive insight possible by embodying abstract truth in symbols.

Rather than hiding truth, the dream asks us to trouble ourselves to learn the language our inner movie producer speaks. We must do the same thing to understand a serious film such as *The Remains of the Day* or *Doctor Zhivago*. The more we grasp a moviemaker's intent, the more complete is our understanding of his or her message.

The key to understanding dream symbols lies in going back inside our experience and asking key questions:

- Where have I seen this entity before?
- What did this object mean to me in the past?
- What does it mean to me right now?
- What meaning does it embody?

Such questions allow us to understand the dream's message.

Linda's dream contained the strange contradiction of Linda trying to save a person who intended to kill her. In addition, she is blamed by the onlookers for the problem. What can we make of the paradoxes?

To help Linda work with her dream, we first suggested that she consider what her giving CPR to her potential murderer might represent. We also asked her to consider why the neighbors were laughing. Were the CPR and the laughter metaphors? Do either of these symbols have any meaning for her relationship with George?

Yes.

One of Linda's lifelong issues has been a struggle with child-hood messages telling her she has no right to exist. Consequently, Linda naturally feels someone is always trying to get rid of her. At the time of the counseling sessions her pending divorce from her husband certainly contained such a message.

To add to her problems, Linda is a chronic rescuer. Even though she means well, Linda creates a lot of her own pain by taking inordinate responsibility for everyone else's life. Linda has a hard time recognizing her tendency to be a savior. Are you getting the dream picture now?

Without going into details of interpretation we will explore in the following chapters, we can quickly spot two important messages in Linda's dream. Her first message was a warning about the futility of trying to rescue someone who is bent on destroying her. Who? Her estranged husband. Second, the neighbors are a clear symbol of her mistake. Linda's dream is trying to help her recognize her self-defeating behavior. The "crowd" is warning her about taking another fall that isn't necessary. Until Linda gets the message, she will have nightly reruns of a painful production as well as set herself up for other spills.

In addition to his insight that dreams embody abstract truth in symbols, Jung also discovered that dreams are essentially compensatory. The dream mechanism helps us gain equilibrium and stay balanced. When we overlook an important portion of our experience or deny an aspect of reality, we start to tilt off-center. The dream compensates for lack of balance by reminding us of the true issues we're not facing.

Paul's dream confronted him with the unproductive way he was relating to his daughter. Although his criticism of her was intended for constructive purposes, an undercurrent was arising from Paul's own unrecognized discontent. His dream was attempting to help him recognize the obvious but unnoticed truth.

Jung also recognized Freud was psychiatrically far too limited in his preoccupation with sex. He believed the drive to find meaning in life is just as significant, if not more so. Jung postulated that no one can become a whole person without a genuine religious experience. He knew many dreams have highly spiritual meaning, and he believed God speaks to people through their dreams.

While many of Jung's religious ideas are not acceptable to the Christian community, his scientific facts help us decipher symbols and understand the language of our inner movie-producing confidante. His discoveries give us a major guideline for dream work.

Opening the Inner Door

A few lessons in "movie talk" will get your interpretation started. Ponder the following four truths, which will help you explore your own symbolic world. These hints will help you decipher your movie producer's best artistic intentions.

1. Scrutinize the Symbols

There is a very significant difference between a sign and a symbol. Signs do not have the capacity to carry the profound ideas and messages that symbols embody. Signs say one thing. Symbols are many-faceted gems that sparkle with meaning and insight.

A sign is one dimensional. For example, a stop sign has no hidden meaning or significant experience to impart. It simply means, "Put on the brakes. Come to a complete halt at this point." You don't get out of the car, run to the pole, hug the sign, and exclaim, "How meaningful!"

A symbol, on the other hand, is multidimensional. Symbols have many layers of truth, each containing its own significance. For example, a wedding ring has profound implications that far exceed its monetary worth. Love, years of personal history, commitment, religious values, family history, and many more experiences are represented by the ring. Anyone who has lost a loved one knows the overwhelming anguish of taking off a wedding ring for the last time. What was once a symbol of joy becomes a reminder of pain and loss.

In Linda's dream CPR was a clear symbol of trying to rescue a needy person. Robert Wise's dream of being left in the field alone expressed abandonment in very graphic terms.

A movie is actually one continuous symbol. We enter a local theater, a darkened room, with a sack of popcorn in hand and prepare to take a symbolic journey. Colored lights are flashed on a white screen while sounds are piped in around the ceiling. If we stop and reflect, we know the whole experience is nothing but an optical and auditory illusion. Yet within a few seconds we are transported across the world, back in time, or hurled into the future. We quickly lose any sense of being in an empty room and are suddenly terrified by lions or horrified by Darth Vader's approaching spaceship. Such is the power of symbols.

While some churches use symbols more than others do, Christians have always recognized the capacity of symbols to communicate the deepest meaning of their faith. Crosses and crucifixes tell the heart of the message without speaking a word. Stained-glass windows and steeples shout to casual passersby. Altars and chalices speak loudly about the problem of sin and the promise of forgiveness.

Symbols depict what would take hours of abstract talk to describe. The more we understand symbols, the more profound is our insight into what they embody. The Nazi swastika immediately tells the story of brutality, despotism, death camps, evil ambition, treachery. The American flag has an opposite effect. Our lives are filled with symbols of varying degrees of importance. The chances are high that you bought your present automobile for symbolic meaning as well as transportation. If you don't think so, just rip off that BMW emblem and let the neighbors think it's only a Chevrolet . . . or maybe a Yugo!

Our dream symbols are so powerful because they take us into a multilayered world where past experience and present needs collide with our hunger for meaning and purpose. Personal hopes and God's intentions form another crossroad out of which dream material arises. Once we understand these summit meetings in our soul, we are changed by the insight. Dream symbols take us to pinnacles of perspective we didn't even know existed.

Our task in deciphering dreams is to discover the many personal meanings and messages these symbols have for us.

2. Set the Symbol Free

The first look at a dream experience almost always gives us the feeling that interpretation is impossible. The whole terrain looks nonsensical and as logical as conversation with the Mad Hatter. We may feel the dream is little more than a trip with Alice to Wonderland. We must put on new lenses. Intuition, not logic, is our best bet in understanding the symbols in our dreams.

Don't misunderstand. We're not suggesting that we shift into irrational thinking; rather, we must become comfortable with our intuitive abilities. We must allow a more profound process than syllogistic logic to work. Similar to hunches and premonitions, intuition allows interpretation to bubble up from within. Here's the point: *The dream is not a puzzle to be solved as much as it is a mystery to be explored.*

Freud's theories erred by being too logical. He saw dream interpretation as being like a diving board. He used the symbol as a starting point from which to take the plunge into what logically followed from his predetermined set of values and ideas. For example, if a person dreamed of a key opening a lock, Freud concluded the dream was about sexual intercourse.

Jung discovered the opposite approach is needed. We must associate *to* the symbol. The approach is more like reading an old high school yearbook and letting memories arise out of the pictures. He suggested we walk around inside the depiction until insight arises out of the symbol itself.

Let's use this approach to go back to Freud's key-and-lock illustration. Such an image might more accurately convey an opportunity to "open up" a new relationship. Perhaps some new truth needs to be "unlocked." Maybe the dream is telling us that we hold in our hands "the key to the future" if we aren't afraid to allow our hidden potential to be "unlocked." We may need to open a memory that has been "locked" shut for a long time. Each of these interpretations could be correct under the right circumstances. Only the context of the dream can tell us. We must set the symbol free to speak its own message.

Linda needed to work on discovering what George represented

in her dream. Her task was to explore what he meant in normal life and try to gain insight as to why, in her dream, he fell out of the car in an unconscious condition.

Later, you will learn a method and insight into how one can let dream symbols release their full potential. At this point, just learn how to let symbols have their voice. Look for layers of meaning.

Let's take another look at your automobile. Ponder why you bought this particular car. Beyond transportation, what meaning do the car's shape, style, color, and model have for you? How does the appearance affect you? Could it convey a message about who you want people to think you are? Is it a statement that you don't care what people think? Your interpretations of meaning might run from your being recognized as having prominence to just being seen as a regular citizen. You might even find the car is a symbol of frustration because the auto is so much less than you want people to think you really are capable of owning.

Now take a look at your desk or bedroom dresser. What pictures, mementos, or keepsakes do you find there? Why are they there? What do they mean to you? What memories do they bring back?

As your mind wanders from one experience to another, you are setting the symbols free to speak. You will find feelings, insights, memories coming to mind. This exercise helps you understand your own symbolic life.

Poetry can help us get the knack of opening the symbolic world. Consider Robert Browning's haunting lines, "Earth is crammed full of heaven, and every common bush aglow with God. Those who see take off their shoes, and the rest pick blackberries." Let the symbol of berry-picking take you on an inner journey. Feel your way into the insight. Have you ever felt yourself missing God because of your preoccupation with mundane things? Sure. Symbols help us remember how such a thing could happen. They also help us learn how to read the insights in our dreams.

3. Dreams Have No Restraints

The movie producer within us is a wild person who will use any means possible to make a statement. The director's approach is a creative no-holds-barred style generally quite different from how we operate in normal life. Remember, dreams are compensatory. In fact, the more conservative you are, the wilder your dreams have to be to compensate for your own reserve. Don't be put off by the strange or the bizarre.

Start by recognizing dreams as facts about which we make no assumptions except that they make sense and are expressions of our unconscious mind. Remember that the dream isn't trying to disguise the message but present the story in pictorial language. To become comfortable with the dream form, we must be willing to meet aspects of ourselves we usually repress. Ninety percent of the time there's nothing wrong with us except that we aren't comfortable with the total truth about ourselves. We tend to take ourselves far too seriously!

4. The Dream Is a Lost-and-Found Department

We've all had an experience of losing a contact lens, a needle, a pair of glasses. We look high and low in great frustration. Once the lost item is found, however, we can't understand why we took so long to see it. It seems so obvious. Dream meanings are of the same order.

The compensatory dream function reminds you where you are off-center. It may take a "far-out form" to "wake you up." For example, a dream of either flying or falling may be a pointed warning that you are overextended and headed for a fall. You are not foretelling the future but listening to your own inner common sense. Don't underestimate the wisdom that resides hidden in your soul!

Paul Meier's dream that pointed him toward the Psalms opened his eyes to a psychological principle he understood academically but had missed in personal practice. He had misplaced an important precept. Linger in the lost and found. You'll find what you don't even know you've lost.

Good News, Bad News

Both Linda and Paul received difficult dream information with extremely important consequences. Arthur Miller's play *After the Fall* depicts the truth that some of the most important tasks we have to complete are also the most painful to perform. No one wants to face up to these throbbing, healing messages, but we can't get well without them.

Our tendency to repress and deny such communiqués creates dreamland. We have no alternative but to open the secrets of the night. In the end, the dream *always* has good news for us.

Are dreams always right? Yes and no.

The dream is correct about how we *feel*. You can count on the dream to tell you the truth about yourself. In a subjective sense, the dream message is always right.

Objective truth is another matter. Dreams tell us "the way things are," not "the way they should be." The only final source of truth is the Bible. Therefore, dream insight and direction must always be tested by the absolute standard found in Scripture.

The dream is a mirror to help you see the back of your head but not a new canon by which to judge empirical reality. However, the message always has positive implications for your life.

Your Assignment

Task 1. Assess the Symbolic Statements in Your Life

To help you get in touch with your own processes of symbolic thinking, we have two assignments for you. Taking a clue from Linda's dream, look around your desk, bedroom, and living room and note what you use to make symbolic statements about yourself. Why do you have certain pictures hung in prominent places? What are they saying about what is valuable, important, and significant in your life? Take a second look at your jewelry. Why do you wear certain items? What messages do the pieces communicate?

Sit down with a piece of paper and make a list of the ways in which you use symbols to paint pictures of what is important to you.

Task 2. Write Your Movie

If someone gave you the money to make a movie of your life, how would you make the film describe who you are? What actors would you select from Hollywood to play the key roles? What colors would you use as dominant hues? What sort of sound track would you use for the background? Classical, western, rock, or contemporary?

To make it even more interesting, what other period in history might you select to tell your story? Could you make your life story into a medieval battle between knights in shining armor, like *El Cid*, or would it be a good old-fashioned western shoot-'em-up?

Sketch out some ideas on a piece of paper and let your imagination have free rein. Simply let the creative juices flow, and make sure you don't censor yourself. What suits your fancy is best!

After you're done with the script, think about the story and how the components are symbolic ways of talking about your feelings, ideas, dreams, and hopes. This material is exactly the stuff your inner dream mechanism wants to use. As you get better at understanding the language, you'll find your dream messages will get much clearer.

And besides, it's a lot of fun.

Chapter 3

GETTING IN
TOUCH
Waking Up to Your Dreams

*Many efforts to direct, predict, or control are in
reality flights from experience of forms of self-
denial. In actuality man is not predictable; man
is forever impermanent. . . . one lives and loves,
suffers, and forgets, and begins again . . .*
CLARK E. MOUSTAKAS, *CREATIVITY AND CONFORMITY*

Sue was mystified by a vivid dream of a snow-covered
mountain with a refrigerator on the top. In the
dream, a little girl is hiding inside and peeking out the cracked door.
The child can see a great frozen lake at the bottom of the mountain.
On top of the frozen lake is a large block of ice. Locked inside the
chunk is the identical twin of the child in the refrigerator.

We can guess Sue is "frozen" at a particularly important place
in her life. As a matter of record, Sue had already gone through one
divorce because she was frigid and sexually dysfunctional. Some
time later another dream forced her to face the issue she judiciously
tried to avoid, emotionally "thawing."

In the second dream, Sue slowly creeps down the stairs of the

29

house where she lived at age sixteen. Suddenly her maternal grandfather enters the room wearing a black Dracula-style cape. He grabs Sue and makes her spread her naked legs apart. Suddenly the grandfather pours acid on her. Sue wakes up screaming.

Reflection helped Sue remember the maternal grandfather had been accused of fondling little girls but she couldn't remember if he ever did such a thing to her. The dream tells Sue, "Look again."

Would any of us want to forget such real-life experiences? Of course! Such inclinations are part of what makes it difficult for us to remember many of our dreams, but far less traumatizing experiences have exactly the same effect. Even though we aren't running from repressed scandal, we still struggle to face normal aspects of our lives that were unacceptable at a past time. We can be just as "frozen" over very common childhood issues that still intimidate us as adults. Therefore, we have compiled some tips on how dreams help us break through our own "ice barriers."

Put on Your Nightcap

Start expecting to receive nightly messages. If you're not convinced you dream every night, here's an exercise to start you remembering. Set the alarm for six hours of sleep. When you awake you should be able to catch the fourth dream of the night. If nothing happens, try an hour earlier or later the next night.

You may protest paying such a price for getting in touch. A few hints to the mind may do the trick. However, dealing with the unconscious side of our personalities means we must operate in terms to which the unseen responds. When someone yells, "Don't touch or you'll get burned!" the conscious mind understands. However, you can shout all day at the unconscious dimension and get nowhere. Ask the out-of-control alcoholic who keeps saying, "I won't take a drink," right up to the moment he or she downs a glass of booze!

Here's an example of how you communicate with symbolic thinking. Consider a wife who is planning a romantic evening at home with her husband. Soft lights, perfume, a soothing ballad on the FM station, a new negligee, and she's on her way much quicker than reading a typewritten statement demanding more personal attention! Like an invitation to affection, you have to set the stage with symbols to invite dreams to come forth.

In the last chapter, we suggested you explore your own symbolic world. Here are a number of additional steps that will help you wake up to your dreams.

Step 1. Get Ready

Half the fun of going to the movies is the preparation—reading the reviews in the paper, studying the advertisements, and reflecting on the mood you're in. You talk about the options with your spouse. Once you're at the theater you tank up on soft drinks and popcorn before settling into just the right seat. By the time the theater is dark, you're ready to enter another world.

In a similar manner, as bedtime approaches, talking about the possibility of a dream with a spouse is what we call a pump primer. If you're alone, reflect on previous meaningful dreams and muse about how important your dreams are to you. You are inviting your inner movie producer to go to work.

Next get prepared to catch the dream when it appears. Maybe you've heard the old story about the unprepared congregation going to a church meeting to pray for rain. One little boy observed no one brought an umbrella! The child understood the contradiction. Failure to put out a pencil and paper reflects the same ambiguity.

Put a pad and pencil on your nightstand. Robert Wise used to have a small reading light he could flip on without disturbing his spouse; now he uses a ballpoint pen with a battery-operated light that shines when the pen is pressed on the paper. The most helpful and comprehensive approach is to have a small tape recorder on the nightstand. Then you can mumble the dream into the machine more easily and with greater detail than writing it out. These actions suggest to your movie producer you mean to pay attention to whatever is ready to roll!

Step 2. Get in the Mood

Since we know highly rational people have more difficulty remembering dreams than do intuitive inner-oriented creative dreamers, we recognize the need to shift into a more reflective posture. It's time to shut off your mathematical professor and let the artist in you come forth.

Listening to mellow, meditative music often helps. Selections can run from the classics to contemporary—whatever makes you "feel" is sufficient. Rather than entertainment, you are seeking a peaceful reflective atmosphere. Sitting down with a book of poems or a meaningful novel has a similar effect.

You may be thinking, "Wait a minute. I've never gone in for that far-out, language-of-the-soul stuff. I don't understand what the artistic talk is all about." Don't be put off. Before you tune out, take the opportunity to discover a side to yourself that your dreams have probably been trying to introduce you to for a long time. Everyone has an inner area where meaning is experienced and his or her deepest feelings reside. Aesthetics are essential to our humanity. Beauty opens the soul. We meet God in this same place.

Poetry speaks the symbolic language. Word pictures get us in touch with the finer and more meaningful aspects of our experience. For example, read Robert Frost's poem, slowly thinking about how it might reflect unexplored aspects of your past.

32

The Road Not Taken

Two roads diverged in a yellow wood,
And sorry I could not travel both
And be one traveler, long I stood
And looked down one as far as I could
To where it bent in the undergrowth;

Then took the other, as just as fair,
And having perhaps the better claim,
Because it was grassy and wanted wear;
Though as for that the passing there
Had worn them really about the same.

And both that morning equally lay
In leaves no step had trodden black.
Oh, I kept the first for another day!
Yet, knowing how way leads on to way
I doubted if I should ever come back.

I shall be telling this with a sigh
Somewhere ages and ages hence:
Two roads diverged in a wood, and I—
I took the one less traveled by,
And that has made all the difference.[1]

As you read the poem, what journeys into the past do you find yourself taking? What symbols of your past life come to mind? What emotions are evoked?

When Paul Meier completed the poem exercise, a surprising dream from age sixteen flashed back. Paul remembered awaking in deep consternation over a dream about a personal transgression. He felt a deep need to square things with God and confess the wrong. The prayer after the dream was a turning point in Paul's life. The personal commitment he made that night guided his life for the next thirty years.

The following day Paul was moved to make another lifetime decision. Rather than continue in his father's footsteps and become a carpenter, Paul concluded he should be a doctor. He wanted to use this training to help people find the same spiritual meaning and commitment he had experienced. He had taken the road less traveled.

Paul's entire life's course was shaped by that one dream.

This process of "mental mastication" will help open up your analytical mind and deepen your dialogue with hidden portions of your personality. Equally important for our purposes in this chapter, you are greasing the hinges so the doors of your unconscious can open. We will explore various exercises to help you become centered within yourself.

Try two conversations as you prepare to go to sleep. Consciously say to yourself, "I really want to remember my dream tonight." Then talk to God. Pray, "Lord, I want to know everything You have to tell me. Please speak in my dreams." Before you know it, the other end of the conversation begins.

Step 3. Don't Fear Letting Go

Childhood developmental experiences universally limit the scope of what we allow ourselves to feel and experience. Our self-imposed restraints keep us from being in touch with important parts of ourselves. Because of these tendencies we dream but have a hard time remembering our dreams.

For example, boys are often taught to avoid or ignore tender feelings and sensitive thoughts. The macho style doesn't allow much room for enjoying flowers or weeping when Bambi's mother gets shot. On the other hand, women may learn to stuff inside them all forms of anger or aggression just as Sue hid the truth about her grandfather's sexual abuse. Because we treat these controversial feelings and tendencies as unacceptable, they disappear from rational examination, only to return in our dreams. Such deeply repressed aptitudes may return in the form of a clown in the dreams of the overly serious or a comedian in the highly controlled person's nightly adventures.

The epigraph by Clark Moustakas that heads this chapter was right! "Many efforts to direct, predict, or control are in reality flights from experience or forms of self-denial."[2] We need to work on *not* censuring our ideas, thoughts, feelings, or beliefs but rather allowing ourselves a full range of emotions.

Please don't misunderstand our intent. We are *not* advocating that you pander licentious impulses or indulge your most base appetite. Rather, we are suggesting the necessity of being honest about the full range of feelings *everyone* has. Your dreams confront you with what's really going on at the core of your being. Denial of the facts about feelings is the problem.

Don't be threatened when some horrendous act or impulse pops up. Because you have a lurid thought or murderous urge doesn't make you an evil person or mean you'd do it. The wonderfully intricate mechanism inside our heads will explore every aspect of human possibility. In fact, these mental exercises keep us from having to go through actual events and suffer the awful consequences.

Contemplating what motivated Lee Harvey Oswald, accused assassin of President John Kennedy, may suddenly cause an animal lover to think of what it would be like to kill a deer, even though the person would never do such a thing. Here is how your mind works:

You see yourself walking into a sporting goods store purchasing a high-powered rifle. Next, you are lurking behind a tree, waiting for Bambi to come into range. Slowly, the .347 is raised to your shoulder. With cold, murderous intent, you squeeze the trigger. *Boom!* The deer flies backward into the forest and tumbles to the ground. For a moment you feel great satisfaction.

But how could you ever consider such a monstrous idea? It is because we are all equipped with the ability to suspend our values temporarily while our imagination takes us on trips to the moon. Murderous impulses are as common as coveting.

Fantasy is one of a writer's most important tools. Ingenuity takes us where we've never been. None of us has to feel guilty about buying a ticket to our own inner wonderland. Paying attention to the ride will tell you what motivates you these days.

If you have trouble connecting with your dreams, ask yourself if you have a tendency to censor yourself. Do you limit any particular set of feelings or thoughts? Try to open up any areas where you impose restraints.

Step 4. Take Every Detail Seriously—But Consider Later

While experiencing the dream you must not evaluate important details and aspects of what is running through your mind. The fact that a house is black instead of white won't seem of consequence until later. Therefore, we must record the dream as completely and as fully as possible without reflection. If we get up to go to the bathroom, the whole experience will probably evaporate like a shimmering soap bubble bursting in the breeze. The instant you awake start making the most comprehensive notes possible.

When learning dream work at the Benedictine Abbey, Robert Wise started paying attention to his dreams for the first time. "The environment was highly conducive to recollection. I quickly found involvement in my dreamscapes to be so total, I assumed the vividness of each aspect would linger. Wrong! If I didn't get the pieces of the puzzle on paper quickly, they vanished like bubbles.

"One particular dream seemed very important but slipped through my fingers because I didn't act immediately. The best I could recall was working in the monastery with panes of glass. Something about the way light came through the glass seemed very important. A lady appeared beside me in a chapel, but I couldn't remember what she said. Only the word *viva* remained. I waited too long with my head on the pillow, enjoying the feeling of the dream, before I tried to write down the details."

Don't evaluate what you've experienced until you've got the reverie on paper. Reflection is as deadly as sunlight in a movie theater. Just concentrate on re-entering the dream sequence. Later, other details may come back to mind. Add these reflections back in.

Several hours after Robert awoke from his "panes of glass" dream, he sat down in the quietness of his room to reflect and tried to re-enter the dream. "Rather than simply remembering, I attempted to experience the flow of the story line again. Several times I revisited the dream, as I would go back over a very enjoyable movie, letting the reels turn again in my head.

"To my surprise, I abruptly realized in the dream I was making a stained-glass window in the monastery shop. Sunlight cast many-colored shadows on my worktable, and I saw an analogy with how prayer brings the light of God into the soul just as stained glass fills a church with beautiful illumination.

"This time, I made myself not think about the implications of what I was encountering. I let the rest of the story flow. The lady in the chapel returned and began to share a message about inspiration. At that moment I understood she was saying, '*Viva vox*.' Instantly, I knew the meaning of the dream.

"During my seminary studies, I was taken with Martin Luther's theory of the inspiration of Scripture he called the *viva vox*, Latin for 'living voice.' Luther taught Scripture was not originally meant to be written down, but spoken. As we hear the Word of God, its work is accomplished in our hearts. He believed Scripture should be heard more than read. The Bible was written down on paper only to accommodate our frailties of memory.

"I realized my dream was an affirmation of my extended periods of prayer each day during worship. I started the day with 6:00

A.M. worship, went to a 4:00 P.M. holy Communion service, ended the day with compline prayer, and probably prayed for at least two hours in between these times. The dream told me these periods of devotion were like the effect of stained-glass windows, creating holy space inside a church, so the voice of God could and would be heard in the souls of the worshipers. The insight was almost overpowering!"

How your dream made you feel as you were awaking is also important. The events in the dream may have looked funny but left you very sad. Or the dream could be tragic but leave you happy. Such contradictions are major clues in deciphering the message. Remember our tendency to censure ourselves has the potential to destroy the message!

Some people seem to dream in color much of the time while others have color only occasionally. Either way, color is very significant. Was it an angry red or a passionate pink? Was green the color of growth or illness? The shade contains vital commentary. Write it down as precisely as possible and expect dreams in color to be unusually important. While most dreams are colorless, intense dreams are often in vivid color.

Your notations are a leash on your dream; they can help you rein the experience back in. Don't wait long to begin. The more quickly you amplify the dream the better. Because Robert Wise uses a typewriter and computer so much, he tries to sit down within thirty minutes and write out the dream as if it were a short story. He *always* types the date at the top of the page. The details are fleshed out and anything that may come to mind is added. However, he avoids forcing a dream or elaborating artificially on what the dream might be triggering as he thinks about it. The goal is to be *faithful and comprehensive.*

Later we'll describe how to make a dream dictionary. You'll find the timing of a dream is often important. For example, dreams on birthdays or New Year's are generally very significant. For the moment, just start keeping track of when the experience occurred.

Once it is on paper, sit back and look at your short story. Does an interesting title come to mind? Let your imagination have a little fun. Put the title at the top. When we learn how to decipher the dream we will discover the title may have important clues for interpretation.

After everything is written down on paper or in the computer, take a few moments to reflect on the events of the previous day that formed a setting for the dream. Was the day traumatic? Did you go to sleep upset? Worried? What problems were weighing on your mind? What did you see on TV? Experience at the movies?

Should you realize the dream is almost a duplication of the late-night thriller on the tube, don't discount the dream as just your own personal rerun. Recognize that the dream producer selected that particular form because of its special ability to convey the hidden message you are failing to comprehend. Chances are high your rerun is saying you're not really paying attention to the message or at least haven't gotten it right yet.

Remember, no detail is too trivial to be recorded. Seemingly obscure portions may turn out to be vital to unlock the riddle. One of the greatest dangers is to let yourself have a preconceived idea about what a symbol or the dream is about. Inevitably we dismiss what we think isn't vital. The result is loss of insight.

Step 5. Learn to Recognize the Structure

Most dreams will naturally fall into four segments, which we outline briefly here as parts one through four. In a subsequent chapter this internal order will be explored in detail. For the time being, acquaint yourself with how the dream develops like a story. Even if the parts don't seem logical to your conscious mind or pieces of the story are strangely disjointed, you can begin to identify how the inner logic of the dream works.

Part 1. The first segment is the *setting*. Dreams begin by dealing with a particular concern. During the first episode, an environment, or setting, is constructed for the message. You can safely identify the first portion as the context.

For example, we began this chapter with Sue's dream. The context, or setting, is a snow-covered mountain with a child in a refrigerator. Something in Sue's life seems to be frozen.

Part 2. The second segment sets up the problem or the situation that needs to be faced. In this portion the dream wants to present an unresolved issue. As the scenery changes out of the setting, we are being introduced into a realm of struggle. This issue is the plot of your dream's story.

Sue's dream is brief but quickly tells us about the problem of a child hiding in an icebox. Refrigerators are dangerous places for children to play. We can immediately see something is wrong with the environment around Sue's life.

Part 3. While it is not always the case, quite often the third segment offers you a "because" transition. The structure of the dream is attempting to give you an important hint about the problem or the solution. If you can identify it, the "because" makes the rest of the dream more obvious.

The "because" in Sue's dream isn't as distinct because the dream is so compact. However, the block of ice sitting on the frozen lake suggests a possible rationale of sorts. Something is wrong because a child is frozen.

Part 4. Finally, the last of the dream is the solution. Dreams always bring good news offering us wisdom we didn't know we possessed. The dream's conclusion will help us deal with the problem or issue we have been overlooking.

Sue needed to free her twin who was encrusted and helpless in the ice. If she could release the alter ego, she would find her own deliverance. Sue's second dream confronted her with painful clues to understand why her emotional world was frozen. The attack of her Dracula grandfather has such obvious sexual overtones we could suspect, but not conclude, Sue may very well have been a victim of sexual abuse sometime in her life, either by her grandfather or by someone he symbolizes.

While the context of sexual abuse is a distinct possibility, we must also be aware that such dreams don't necessarily mean participation. As a psychiatrist, Paul is quick to offer the reminder that childhood fears and fantasies can create a false memory syndrome. Accusing a grandfather or a father purely from dream evidence can be a serious miscarriage of justice. Dream evidence needs to be only the first step in establishing a problem. Verification by other supporting material must follow.

For the moment don't worry about the content of your dream messages. Just get acquainted with your internal hieroglyphics so you're in a position to use what will follow.

Step 6. Keep a Notebook

In a subsequent chapter, we will explore how dreams build on each other. In addition, we will explore how symbols take on wider and more profound meaning as they are repeated in dreams. We have found most people develop a definite set of symbols that are used many times in many ways. Therefore it's very helpful to keep tabs on what you have dreamed in the past.

For years, Robert Wise has kept a notebook of all the dreams he has recorded, amplified, and deciphered. The dreams are filed by date. In the front of the notebook is an index of dreams' symbols with the date at the side. This method allows for quick access to what the symbol meant in previous years or at more recent times. This index looks something like this:

A

airplane	exaltation	Jan. 9, '83, April 11, '84, June 16, '93
altar	place of awe, catharsis	May 20, '85, Feb. 11, '92
animals	great strength	Oct. 13, '83, Mar. 14, '85, Dec. '94

B

| band | performance | Jan. 20, '83, Jan. 13, '84, May 10, '89 |
| bargains | conserving the past old values | Mar. 8, '87, Nov. 1, '89 |

The alphabet index runs clear through zebra!

After more than a decade of recordings, the material is incredibly rich and profoundly helpful to Robert in getting in touch with the many streams flowing through his life. In addition, this depth of attention gives powerful impetus to the dream process. The more one honors dreams, the better they come.

Your Assignment

Task 1. Start Getting Familiar with the Process

Many people have a very limited sense of their dream world. Generally they're the ones who need the inner journey the most.

Here's a word of encouragement. Be good to yourself and start gently. Learning to listen to your night messages may take some time. Let it come piece by piece. One step leads to another. The suggestions in this chapter are priming the pump, setting the stage for reception. Use them and see what happens tonight.

Become comfortable with the idea of learning new insights about yourself. Don't worry about discovering some dastardly secret about your childhood. Rather, anticipate learning how to accomplish the things you would pray for in your life. The most joyous and stimulating perceptions will pop up left and right. Dreams are fun.

Task 2. Don't Place Expectations on Yourself

Let your dreams come without worrying about missing some detail or spectacular message. If you didn't get the point of one night's insights, remember you've got the rest of your life to work on the project. The message will be back in an even more intriguing form tomorrow night.

If all you remember is a little piece of something, play with the fragment. More will come as you mull over what's at hand. Awareness grows as we practice alertness.

Avoid the trap of overly spiritualizing common sense. Everything coming up from the bottom is not in the same class as Jacob's dream at Bethel or Joseph's dream about the birth of Jesus. Just because you dream about a certain person or a certain city doesn't mean God is telling you to marry that person or move to that city. At this point we're starting on a journey. Just have a good time getting prepared for the trip.

How much time should you devote to dream work?

How much time do you have . . . to grow spiritually and become a whole person? It's your call! People tell us they barely have time for five minutes of prayer a day. Usually they are the same folks who put in a couple of hours in front of the tube every evening. How about dropping the sitcoms in favor of personal growth and more conversation with God?

Couldn't you get more out of studying the Bible instead of doing dreams? Would you get more out of Bible reading when you need to see a marriage counselor? Obviously, you need both. Spiritual development isn't "either/or" but a "both/and" proposition. Let's not mix apples and oranges.

You may go for days and not record or work on a dream. At other times the need for dream study is urgent. The problem isn't how much time you have; the issue is your readiness to work on spiritual development. Don't get compulsive, just concerned.

Are you ready? Hang on. Here we go!

Chapter 4

TUNING IN
Thinking Symbolically

The boy could see how the Hitler force rose within him, making him feel strong and powerful when he was really overpowered by Hitler. Seeing Hitler as a power that took possession of him, he could disidentify from him and see a self that could oppose him, a self that could choose between the forces of good and evil in the conflict within the psyche.
FRANCES G. WICKES, *THE INNER WORLD OF CHOICE*

We are not one person but the compilation of many selves. While we try to present one particular face to the public and often insist people recognize this "us" as who we truly are, we know we have an appearance for friends and a face for the family. At work we can be quite different than we are at play. This highly diverse assortment of appearances is not an indication of mental illness. To the contrary, such performances are the norm of human behavior. In fact, we need many options to maintain stability.

Ancient Greeks called our many faces *personas*. Today the historical remnant is Thespian masks hanging on theater walls. One face frowns; the other smiles. The first actors changed masks during plays to signal shifts in mood. The Greeks knew our everyday personas change like the wind reversing from north to south.

Comparable to a collection of hats assembled over many, many decades, we develop our own ensemble of masks of infinitely more complex variety than simply happiness and sadness. Our assortment of interchangeable faces remains hidden just behind our foreheads. Upstairs in our mind's compartments, where the little people who run our mental computers live, we keep our secret assortment of special appearances and carefully structured facial effects. As mood and social occasion change, our internal helpers get the correct "look" in place.

Deceived by Our Deception

However, the problem is we don't use the masks to accurately reflect what we are feeling. Quite the opposite! The persona's value is camouflaging what is truly going on in our mind. The name of this game is *deception*. Our happy face may actually conceal disappointment and anger. The sad mask is often used to avoid admitting glee over someone's misfortune. And so it goes, hundreds of times each day.

But don't feel defensive! Our masquerades can be necessary and helpful on many occasions. We never endorse dishonesty, but propriety and appropriateness demand we not express our true feelings publicly in many situations. Complete transparency would put us at the mercy of unscrupulous people who could use our honesty against us. In addition, we need time to digest first impressions before we decide if our initial feelings are correct. Our social masks buy us a respite.

However, the problem emerges when we lose sight of our own

deceptiveness. We may mistake a mask as a true representation of our inner self. We start "wearing" the error on the outside. One generation dresses like hippies; another always comes as yuppie business executives. Both are caricatures. They have forgotten that appearance is not the reality.

Some of us may feel we *must* wear one face all the time regardless of what our true emotions are. Childhood development will not allow us to step outside of a particular mold our parents forced on our personalities. Our range of emotional responses has been diminished to fit the perimeters of a very limited persona.

Learning to Read the Clue Cards

In each of these examples we have taken on a "symbolic existence." Appearance is mistaken for fact. We have been swallowed by a role we are playing. We are unfortunate caricatures of the real person God intended us to be.

Once we become aware of this behavior we can better understand how our dreams are similar symbolic statements about who we are. Just as we play charades, the dream puts on a production for us to view. In fact, the cast of characters is often trying to show us a problem with our current social facade. The dream uses the lie to make us see the truth.

Take a second look at the universal human tendency to have many personas. We began by noting it is normal human behavior to jump back and forth between quite diverse representations of who we are. However, *normal* isn't the same as *desirable*. The truth is we need to strive for greater personal integration, minimizing the need for fragmentation. The major goal of our little movie producer is to help us become more whole by expressing our inner divisions.

And just who or what is the movie producer? Sorry. We don't have a complete or definitive answer. Many scientific sources consider the dream mechanism to be like other aspects of our mental and emotional makeup. Similar to fear, anger, and passion, we are simply born with the capacity. Other thinkers such as Morton Kelsey believe the movie director is actually the Holy Spirit.

We aren't even vaguely suggesting or implying the movie director is a spirit guide or some other form of independent spiritual reality. Our term—movie director—is a neutral way of explaining a natural phenomenon.

While we are not pushing any particular theory, we suggest dreams operate much like the conscience and are a natural part of who we are. While the conscience can be wrong or distorted, it has an indisputably valuable function in helping us discern right from wrong. The Holy Spirit works through and uses the conscience. Similarly, dreams aren't infallibly right, but God has chosen to work in and through them just as He does with our sense of right and wrong. Consequently, *movie producer* is used to describe the direction and insight that comes both from God and us.

Hitler and Other Monsters

Let's explore some of the ways in which fragmentation and inappropriate personas create problems for us. As we see the problem more clearly, we will also understand better how our dreams try to straighten us out by using similar symbolic tools.

In *The Inner World of Choice,* Frances Wickes describes a nine-year-old boy troubled with a violent temper. Often his rage resulted in cruelty. He felt as if a Hitler lived inside him. The imaginary Hitler seemed to be growing in power, forcing the child into even worse behavior. A persona was conquering the boy.

As Wickes helped the child develop a dialogue with the shadow side of his personality, the destructive urge was brought under control. His real enemy was not his mother, teachers, or friends, but himself. Slowly the boy began to see how the destructive urges made him feel more powerful but were actually taking over his life. The child started recognizing he had the capacity to disidentify himself from this persona. He could choose the good rather than the evil. The boy's true self really was stronger than he realized.[1]

We had a similar client in Dallas, Texas, with recurrent dreams he was Hitler. George's consuming dreams were so overpowering he concluded he had experienced reincarnation; George believed he had received the soul of Hitler! His conclusion was terrifying and was the source of great anxiety. He was about to accept as fact the horrifying notion Adolf Hitler was taking over his body.

In contrast to his friends' sloppy jeans, George appeared to have stepped out of the latest fashion catalog. To the casual eye, George and his family were the upper-class elite with philanthropic instincts and little in common with the Nazis!

Once work was begun on his dreams, a number of George's tendencies became clear. Actually, he was a rather rigid person who tried to run his personal world like a dictator runs the government. His high-fashion clothes were a uniform of sorts. Appearances to the contrary, he had a significant capacity for deception and manipulation. Later, members of his family proved to be quite malicious people who spread gossip and specialized in character assassination, even following people around town like SS spies! George's preppie world wasn't the complete picture at all. His dream revealed a ruthless strain running through both George's personality and family.

The dreams were attempting to bring to George's attention an unfortunate aspect of his personality. His Hitler mask was a jolting but appropriate way to wake up George to the meaning of his smugness and to face his potential for being a conniving diabolical person. He needed to learn to use "symbolic thinking" for, rather than against, himself.

Puns, Ploys, and Poetry

The inner movie producer's job is to help us do the same thing—use our "symbolic thinking" for, rather than against, ourselves. He uses every tool possible to "wake us up." For example, the producer is an extraordinary comedian and punster. There is no limit to the humor used in dreams. Clever twists of imagery and the turn of a phrase can convey a profound idea. Once you get acquainted with how the symbolic gimmicks work, you'll be amazed at how they clarify the dream's message.

For example, consider these common colorful phrases:

"A wolf in sheep's clothing"
"Ships that pass in the night"
"Bridge over troubled water"
"Missing the bus"
"Getting in hot water"
"Going through the roof"

Each of these symbolic colloquialisms implies a page of explanations. The image is the vehicle of communication. Once you begin to recognize how you actually think symbolically all the time, you will see the way dream structures generally operate.

Let's create a few dreamscapes to see this principle in operation. While you slumber away, a monstrous wolf appears at your door. To your surprise he is quite friendly and wants to help you. You notice the wolf is wearing a fleece-lined jacket and expensive wool pants. Upon awaking you are struck by the fact that the dream is so contradictory. A dangerous wolf wants to be a friend; he is a wolf in sheep's clothing. The clue calls you to look back through your relationships and see if someone offering help may be an enemy in disguise.

The next night you are watching two sail-bedecked schooners plowing through the ocean. With the full moon in the sky, the sea is unusually romantic. As you watch the boats silently glide past, you feel deep regret. Upon awaking you find yourself in a panic but you can't pinpoint what is amiss.

On the basis of what you've learned this far, what might you explore? Look up from the page before you read any further and ponder the idea. No, don't cheat by trying to look at the next several lines.

Did it occur to you that a very special person might be slipping away from you? Could you be about to lose a meaningful relationship with the potential of lifelong consequences? Are your ships passing in the night?

Think about how many colorful phrases you use every day: "going down the drain," "take the bull by the horns," "pulling my leg," "blown away," "skating on thin ice," "dead as a doornail." Taken out of context, none of these phrases would make sense. And of course, when the dream uses such images in a setting we don't understand, they aren't any more recognizable. Should these word pictures be turned into actual depictions, strange images would result, yet the message could be the same as the cliché. Dreams often operate around just such imagery.

One of Paul Meier's clients brought a dream loaded with powerful symbolic significance. Casey kept dreaming she was stuck in a huge trash compactor. After considerable struggle, the young woman was able to get out. The dream ended.

Let the image roll around in your mind for a few moments. See yourself inside a garbage bin as big as your room. The sides start slowly closing in on you. What are you feeling? What might the dream be telling you? What suggestions would you offer to Casey?

Paul's client was the youngest of five children. Her stepfather was a physically and verbally abusive alcoholic. Casey often described her stepfather's childhood treatment as making her feel like trash. One component in her therapy was confronting an eating disorder. Casey was gradually beginning to see how she used food as a substitute for love.

In light of the additional information, how would you interpret the compactor dream?

Paul helped Casey recognize how past circumstances were "putting the squeeze" on her. The eating disorder was part of the destructive pressure bearing down and working against her recovery. On the other hand, therapy was Casey's way of crawling out of the compactor. She had to recognize she wasn't "trash." Her dream ended with good news. Casey was escaping!

Getting the hang of how images work?

Tying Down the Theme

Take a look at the political cartoons in your local paper. You will notice how skillfully the cartoonist depicts a current issue or controversy in the symbols he or she uses. Dogs with politicians' heads may be chasing the president. International leaders are pictured as clowns. After an election, the losers are drawn with their feet sticking out of garbage cans as John Q. Citizen looks on, saying, "Good riddance!" Very quickly you discern what the editorial policy of the paper is on particular matters.

In the same manner you can detect the themes, or motifs, in your dreams and state them in a brief sentence. The more you play with this approach, the better you will become at seeing what is going on.

We suggest you write down every dream you can and begin to collect them in the manner described in the last chapter. In a short while you will have plenty of material to work on. After you have stated what you feel is the central thrust of the dream, write out the issue this theme raises for you.

The following list shows a group of examples from Robert Wise's dream journal:

Motif: I am in a church filled with people playing silly games. They seem to be making fun of me.

Issue: Am I kidding myself about what is really going on in my religious life these days? Is my work at the church filled with foolishness?

Motif: I am driving around with Joseph Stalin, who tells me he doesn't want anyone to know he's there.

Issue: Am I acting like a dictator and not aware of my effect on other people?

Motif: I am in a parade marching with a band and trying to play several different instruments at the same time but having a difficult time keeping up.

Issue: Am I trying to do too many things at once right now?

These exercises in symbolic thinking will help you read your dreams.

Let's Play with a Dream

Possibly one of the most instructive ways to learn dream work is by observing how it's done. Using the insights of the previous chapters, Robert Wise will show you how he dissects one of his favorite dreams and demonstrate how to use symbolic thinking. Here's the dream as he first experienced it:

"I am with a movie producer who makes religious films, and

I'm trying to select a film. The filmmaker is a flashy Hollywood clone with a rather phony aura. Selections are being offered by introducing the actors who played in the movie. The actors come out one at a time from behind a curtain and try to impress me with their performance. Each tries to interest me in the roles he or she plays. The actors are so obnoxious I am turned off by every suggestion. I begin looking in a newspaper to get another description of other movies.

"Suddenly the scene changes, and I am in a hospital room near a woman with cancer. I am with the doctor and the hospital administrator. The doctor tells the administrator the woman will sue over her care. He suggests all assets be put into escrow until the problem is settled. We discuss this pending action.

"Abruptly the scene is gone, and I know the title of the selection I should make is *Hot Fudge Drapes*. The idea of edible draperies occurs to me. The dream is over."

How's that one for starters? Sound like Robert has really lost his grip on reality? Let's see what sense we can make out of the nonsense:

While the "because" factor isn't quite so obvious at the outset, the dream is easily divisible into three segments:

The Setting: Robert's encounter with the movie producer and actors provides the initial framework for the dream. He seems to be looking for the right film or production by considering the roles actors played.

The Problem: When Robert shows up in the hospital there is not only a sick woman but also a pending lawsuit. Looks like trouble!

The Solution: Robert has a vivid but bizarre suggestion for a solution to this whole story. *Hot Fudge Drapes!*

Before Robert settled on this diagram, he took another approach to the scene from another angle. Here's an alternative to pull the content of the dreams apart:

The Setting: Robert meets a rather phony movie producer who, upon closer inspection, reminds him of an evangelical producer of religious films. He is urging Robert to select a film.

The Problem: The actors in the film are trying to impress Robert. Each one is trying to get him to "buy" who he or she is, that is, to choose his or her role. Robert doesn't like what he sees. In fact, he's so turned off he begins to look in the paper to see what else is showing.

The Because: Robert goes to a place that helps people get well. He meets the man who runs the rehabilitation center and a healer. He is also introduced to a woman with both cancer and an attitude problem.

The Solution: Robert is told by a voice outside of himself that the answer to the movie selection he should make is *Hot Fudge Drapes.*

What's the right way to figure out the dream? Possibly you're bothered because Robert didn't slavishly follow his own model. *There's no one right way!* We are not solving a math problem but studying a painting. We seek insight, not formulas. Therefore, whatever brings understanding is valid.

Remember, deciphering a dream is a matter of invoking *insight.*

Often the deeper meaning of a dream pops into our minds long after we have quit working on it. These answers arise from the intuitive side of our brains, not the analytical portions. Solutions come in the form of "aha's" rather than the "Elementary, Watson, elementary," deductive path to truth.

Trying to Find the Yellow Brick Road

This dream was so bizarre Robert had to take a number of turns in the road before he knew he was going down the right path. Because the dream attempts to tell us something we can't face, our own deceptiveness is generally a source of significant detours.

Using both dream diagrams, Robert started walking back into the dreamscape. As always he placed a date at the top of the page to recognize the dream's timing in his life. Later he discovered timing was one of the most important considerations in getting the right direction. He wrote "Hot Fudge Drapes" at the top of the page as a title. It looked really absurd!

Wrestling with the theme wasn't easy because the dream jumped from a movie story to a hospital. Initially, Robert couldn't identify a theme. In fact, the whole dream seemed rather impenetrable.

He had no alternative but to start working on the meaning of the setting. However, he knew his method of going from setting to problem to solution would give him a methodical way to break into his symbolic thinking. Once one gets the setting right, a direction will follow.

Robert decided to go with his four-part analysis. He set up his work page by listing the components down the page. The layout helped him separate the components. He left space on the right side for writing out meaning and insights. Take a look:

Feb. 18, 1982
Hot Fudge Drapes

The Setting:
CHARACTERS (Space left for conclusions about meaning.)
    movie producer

56

"I"
selecting a film
The Problem:
CHARACTERS
actors
negative impact of actors
use newspaper to find alternatives

The Because:
CHARACTERS
hospital scene
sick woman; cancer
doctor
hospital administrator
pending lawsuit
put assets in escrow

The Solution:
CHARACTERS
hot fudge drapes

Once Robert's dream was dissected on paper, he prepared to look carefully at each of the individual parts. A large amount of space was left on the right side of the page so he could write his discoveries as he gained insight into each of the components of the dream.

"Because selecting a movie was an important motive in the dream, I began by asking what cinema meant to me," Robert said. "The answer came quickly. As a movie buff I see at least one flick a week. Once the lights go down, the film transports me into another reality. God has graciously given me the wonderful gift of imagination. I get completely lost in a great film. The whole experience becomes my reality of the moment. Movies offer me another vicarious existence, taking me inside roles actors play and to roles I can never visit.

"From this insight I quickly saw the meaning of the movie producer in my dream. Producers make entry into other worlds possible. However, in my dream I was reminded of a particular small-time producer who made rather awful low-grade religious films. This religious-film producer dresses and acts like a flashy Hollywood-and-Vine type straight out of the forties. He is a shoddy caricature of the real thing. Moreover, his films are bad art. I have no doubt the man's religious motives are high, but his work is artificial and contrived.

"Slowly I began to see how the dream symbolically depicted my search for a personal alternative reality. I was seeking to find a new world of sorts but the whole quest was a religious phony, just like my producer friend. The setting for my dream was a desire to get out of my current real-life world into a different place."

As the insights came, Robert wrote them in simple form across from each of the components of the setting listing on his work page. On the back of the sheet he wrote more elaborate descriptions so he would have the material for later reference. His page now looked like this:

---

movie producer   movie: alternative lifestyle

producer: someone phony

select film   personal quest for life change

These initial discoveries made it much easier to work on the problem segment of the dream. Robert could see the actors were offering him new alternatives by suggesting that he take on different "roles," just as actors play parts. He seemed to know the whole idea would be nothing more than another lousy production like the producer made all of the time. He was confronted with bad acting. What might appear to be a good idea was actually just a fraud.

But Robert couldn't see how the dream's message applied to him. He has an enormous dislike for pretentiousness. Nothing would have less appeal to him than acting a "role" that wasn't authentic. He knew he was going the right way, but he couldn't see the point. The best he could write was:

actors	phony roles

Robert jumped to the solution section of the work page to see how these ideas might converge with new scenery and make the big point. The hospital symbol was fairly easy. Hospitals are places for recovery. Robert already knew something was sick at the movies!

Generally when men dream of women they are touching the feminine or feeling side of their personalities. The woman was telling Robert something cancerous, something malignant, was growing in his feeling world. He needed to let the "healers" work or there wouldn't be a cure for the problem.

In fact, the feeling side of Robert's inner life wasn't going to stand for quackery. Any artificial solutions would be met with violent protest. Robert added these insights to his work page:

hospital	need for healing
woman	my feeling component
cancer	the problem has a malignant, spreading quality
doctor, administrator	healers are needed

Only then did Robert notice that the "escrowed assets" hadn't been considered as an important symbol to be explored. Since this symbol was the "because" part of the dream, it should help develop insight into why he had a problem. Clearly, he was not listening well to something his feeling side was trying to communicate. In addition, some of his best assets were to be kept carefully preserved if he was going to solve this problem. But what assets?

Earlier in this chapter we suggested the date was a major factor in understanding Robert's dream. At this point Robert sat back in his chair, surveyed the dreamscape, and asked himself, "What is going on in my life?" Slowly he realized he was at a more significant point than he would have thought!

"Three days earlier I had returned from an extended sabbatical leave at the Benedictine monastery doing research on the meaning of the soul," he said. "For weeks my life had been immersed in quiet solitude and prayer. Each day at the monastery, many hours had been spent—not just reading about but actually spent—in profound prayer and meditation. During this time I had received many, many extraordinary spiritual encounters with the Holy Spirit. I was truly shaken to the core.

"When I came out of seclusion I was profoundly changed. Noise overwhelmed me. The chatter of idle conversation was almost painful. I watched people race down streets going nowhere. I was appalled at the mindless, soulless lifestyle on every side of me. Television was banal, boring, and deadening. My inner world had gone through a conversion of sorts.

"I felt different, and I thought differently. I was spiritually different. I *was* different. Therefore maybe I should look different. I was bothered by the idea that maybe I should even dress in a more appropriate way to reflect the new orientation. What would it be like to don the traditional robes of a follower of Saint Francis?

Without fully realizing the impact, I had a problem of how to symbolically express my persona."

Finding the Emerald City

The date of the dream was the tip-off. Three days after returning to so-called civilization, Robert had an image problem. He didn't know which face to put on for the public. Should Robert Wise look like a Benedictine monk, a Franciscan friar, or what? His dream was trying to tell him to sort out the options.

"Everything fell into place!" Robert said. "In my quest for the right persona I was going down the wrong road. If I tried to make people think I had become a 'holy man,' I would be as big a phony as my movie producer and his bad actor friends.

"The whole idea of looking or acting special needed a trip to the hospital. I was giving cancer to my emotions. Instead of being real, I was actually becoming more and more artificial. The dream was telling me that my true assets as a person needed to be protected. The answer was to be found out of my own past.

"At that moment I suddenly realized the meaning of *Hot Fudge Drapes*. The insight came so quickly, I didn't even need to elaborate.

"I grew up with a wonderful grandmother who could 'make do' with anything. She was the master of taking old things and making them look brand-new. Her specialty was curtains. No need to re-buy when Grandmother could take yesterday's rags and make them look like tomorrow's treasure. Consequently, I didn't like to buy draperies when we moved into a new house. My inclination was to figure out some way to use the old ones more creatively. See where I'm going?

"Hot Fudge? I play a little game with myself. Ninety percent of the time I avoid the banana split counter because the calories love me even more than I love them. Ice-cream toppings are my fat-producing nemesis. *But* . . . when I've been a good boy (like finishing the writing of a book) I go down for a hot fudge sundae as my special reward to myself. Hot fudge is a synonym for giving myself a treat.

"And there was the meaning of putting my assets into escrow. I needed to hang on to what I had formerly valued. My former personality traits were still assets. The dream was telling me that I didn't need a radical new lifestyle change or alteration of appearance. In fact, I must avoid exterior adjustments which would be phony. The last thing I needed was to start acting in some pseudo-religious role."

If he would just make do with what he'd been in the past, the real Robert Wise would be a treat. Conserve the old ways, and they will become a reward! Robert's dream saved him many embarrassing moments!

Your Assignment

This chapter has been an exercise in learning how to tune in to the world of symbolic thinking. Even though everyone does so all the time, most of us aren't aware of how pervasive the process is. The biggest problems in unraveling dreams generally happen to people who are too literal, concrete, and unimaginative in their approach to life.

Go back and re-read the description of how Robert Wise dissected his dream. Make sure you "feel" the way the process operated. Then take one of your own dreams and follow his guidelines in taking your dream apart. Let your imagination soar. Insight is ahead.

Remember, no interpretation of your dream should lead you to contradict Scripture—the most obvious place the Holy Spirit guides and leads us.

Chapter 5

THE WINDMILLS
OF YOUR MIND
Interpreting the Pieces
in the Puzzle

A man is never the same for long. He is continu-
ally changing. He seldom remains the same for
even half an hour. We think that if a man is called
Ivan he is always Ivan. Nothing of the kind. Now
he is Ivan, in another minute he is Peter, and a
minute later he is Nicholas, Segius, Matthew. . . .
You know that Ivan cannot do a certain thing. . . .
Then you find he has told a lie and you are sur-
prised. . . . And, indeed, Ivan cannot lie; it is
Nicholas who lied. . . . You will be astonished when
you realize what a multitude of these Ivans and
Nicholases live in one man. If you learn to observe
them there is no need to go to a cinema.
P. D. OUSPENSKY, *IN SEARCH OF THE MIRACULOUS*

So what's been happening on *your* dream front lately?
The last chapter challenged you with the task of

taking your own reveries apart. Getting the hang of dream work? We hope insight is starting to flow.

Our most important discovery is recognizing how objects can represent feelings, meaning, and needs. The next step is to find exactly the right association for the symbols. For example, a child could be a representation of our past, or of the promise of our future. Childhood memories are both the happiest and the saddest experiences of life. The spin makes a world of difference.

Remember Robert's dream of abandonment in a field? The interpretation of the recurring dream depended on the meaning of the child. The dream begged a couple of important questions: After years of reappearing, why didn't the child grow up? What significance was embodied in the forever three-year-old child?

As Ouspensky reminds us with his illustration of Peter, Nicholas, and Segius, etc., we often seem to be a fragmented conglomerate of many personalities. The origin of the crowd living in the singularity of our personality comes from our childhoods.[1]

Robert's abandonment dream offered him an important opportunity to sort out this dimension of his personality. People often remark that Robert is a very complex person. While he would gladly opt for the life described in the Shaker hymn, "'Tis a Gift to be Simple," the possibility disappeared before he was six years old! The dream offered some of the reasons for his complex personality.

After working on the implications of the child left in the field, Robert began to see how a very important portion of his childhood had not been integrated into his adult life. The little child of the past had an independent life of his own. He was seeking—searching through the wilderness of Robert's unconscious mind for a place of security and belonging. Periodically the child would surface and demand attention or even take charge of making decisions. He was an invisible factor in Robert's emotional life. The child was still living in Robert's adult life with all of the fears and misgivings of a three-year-old left to survival in the wilds.

Using some of the techniques to be described in this and later chapters, Robert was able to get in touch with this fragment of his past. Robert's dream work taught him the necessity of finding the child lost in his unconscious and making friends with him. The result was extraordinarily healing.

One of Paul Meier's clients, Susan, discovered that the setting for some of her significant dreams was a restaurant. However, the symbol didn't seem to mean anything. Only after working on a number of dreams did Susan really zero in on the message in this context. Her childhood hometown had a limited number of very nice restaurants. Susan realized that eating out had been a special childhood experience that always made her feel important. As she analyzed her restaurant dreams, Susan discovered that nice dining rooms were either a symbol of feeling important or of needing an ego boost. The exact definition brought a wave of new insight. She only needed to know which way the windmills of her mind were turning!

With these insights in mind, we're ready for the next lesson. Let's follow one of our client's dream trails. Tom's breakthrough came as the right associations in his dream brought profound insight into his current life situation.

Tom was reaching a critical point in his therapy. He knew the time had come to make profound and significant decisions. And yet . . . yet . . . he couldn't bring himself to face basic issues that kept him in a state of agitation. Depression returned, and life filled up with torment. In order to achieve a breakthrough, we suggested Tom pay careful attention to his dreams. The next morning he brought the following dream for interpretation.

Tom read his notes for a minute, then began to explain. "I need to make a trip out of town, but my truck is in questionable operating condition and has been so for some time. I've been avoiding small repairs just to get by. I know if I take the truck I will have big problems. Yet I start on the trip."

During earlier therapy sessions, Tom had talked about getting rid of his old pickup. For reasons he couldn't identify, Tom just didn't want to part with the broken-down jalopy. The truck seemed to be like an old pair of shoes or a worn coat, filled with comforting memories of better days.

Tom continued, "The next thing I know, I'm being pulled into a service station repair building. I'm half in and half out of the building. Plenty of tools are available, but I'm hesitant to use them without permission of the owner. I go ahead and start working on the truck to save money. The garage owner is friendly, and he offers me any replacement parts I might need. However, I discover the cost on the bag of parts is fifty-one dollars. I immediately feel I'm being overcharged. I'm in a dilemma on how to proceed. Do I pay, or risk not actually getting the truck fixed well enough to get me where I need to go?"

Tom's description of his vacillation in repairing the truck had a very familiar ring. Over the period of the last six months, he had reflected on his problems in very similar terms.

"I must decide between no solution or a short-term answer," he had said. "I'm paralyzed, not knowing what to do. Temporary repairs will only keep me in the problem. And yet as I'm paying for the repairs, I'm aware I'm paying to stay in the problem. Something in me just doesn't want to let go of the old truck. It's actually inexpensive, but one of my brothers told me to sell it. The last three years have caused me to have strong emotional ties to the truck.

"Suddenly I notice a locust on the window. I am reminded of my sister sharing the Scripture passage, '[He] will restore to you the years that the swarming locust has eaten.'[2] The locust flies away, and the prelude to the opera *Parsifal* is being played."

Tom knew the dream was extremely important in helping him get on with his therapy, but he couldn't get started in deciphering the meaning. He needed something similar, a basis of comparison to start making sense out of the experience.

How can we help Tom read the dream symbols with the necessary accuracy to help him profit by this experience? We must find a form that will assign the correct meaning to the many parts in the dream. We must slow down the windmills of his mind so he gets some control over the messages spinning out. Just as he needed gadgets and devices to fix his dream truck, Tom also needed tools to take the dream apart. We offered a method to give more precise meaning to such images as trucks, garages, mechanics, and locusts.

Paradigms for the Perplexed

Complex, abstract ideas become understandable when we are able to find analogies that explain their meanings in more concrete terms. For example, we say the heart is like a pump and the brain is comparable to a computer. X-ray machines take pictures, and radar shoots electronic bullets. Drugs "blow" people's minds while candy bars "energize" us. We get "juiced" by rock-'n'-roll music, but get "mellow" while listening to Montovani. We use these colorful words to make complex concepts manageable in simpler form.

We must go a step further to find a more comprehensive way to explain large segments of our experience, particularly when systems of thought are involved. These patterns and models are called *paradigms*. Such explanations are like glasses worn to bring everything into focus. We can talk about how a particular paradigm explains our common experience and conveys understanding. Such models of reality develop and enlarge insight.

No paradigm is perfect. Each model is relative to a time in history or a unique philosophy. As decades pass, we explain the same thing in very different ways. The medieval three-story theory of the universe was destroyed by Columbus's voyage around the world. Newton's explanation of gravity based on an apple falling from a tree gave way to Einstein's theory of relativity, $E=MC^2$. The divine right of kings turned into a people's democracy. Our view of reality alters as the world changes.

Actually, several very different paradigms may be needed to explain the same thing. We don't really see a mountain completely unless we travel in a wide circumference looking at a number of sides of the slopes. In the same way very different paradigms can throw greater light on the same phenomenon.

Few fields have had as many abrupt changes of perspective and approach in such a short time as psychotherapy and psychiatry have undergone in the last fifty years. Each new pattern, prototype, and explanation has deepened our insight into how we function. This deepening insight is especially important for understanding dreams.

From Vienna to Zurich

Modern dream interpretation begins with the paradigms developed by Sigmund Freud. As noted previously, Freud believed the dream was trying to hide meaning from us. His preoccupation with sexual explanations for the underlying motives behind behavior caused him to find sexual symbols in all dreams.

From his psychoanalytic couch in Vienna, Freud developed methods of interpretation centered around explanations such as the Oedipus complex, the Electra complex, and the castration complex. While Freud's work stimulated great popular interest in dreams, few people found his paradigms very helpful. His methods often made analysts sound like witch doctors talking mumbo jumbo.

One of the problems with Freud's work was his tendency to impose his preconceived model of personality onto dreams. His ideas of *ego, id,* and *superego* were used as grids through which the dream experience had to pass. Rather than letting the dream speak, Freud tended to become a ventriloquist.

The next great leap forward came with Dr. Carl Jung's analysis of thousands of dreams. In Zurich, Switzerland, Jung systematically cataloged a multitude of images and symbols, discovering the commonality of a great many of the universal icons. When people dreamed of houses, kitchens, bathrooms, bedrooms, cars, or their parents, Jung found they tended to have a strong similarity of meaning. His insights started cracking the dream code in a new and profound way.

Recently, medical research has discovered why Freud was wrong and Jung was right. Studies in the physiology of dreams demonstrated that the unconscious mind is not a jungle of wild passions but a very cohesive system of systematic mental processes. The research of Dr. Jonathan Winson concluded, "Dreams are not disguised as a consequence of repression. The unusual character is a result of the complex associations that are culled from memory."[3] Jung's conclusions were in accord with how memory processing occurs.

From his dream discoveries, Jung was able to develop a new and unique way of looking at the entire personality. He allowed dreams to have full voice, telling us whatever they felt we should know. Consequently Jung's dream discoveries gave us new understandings of how personality functions.

Jung's view of personality included the meaning of the soul. He believed religious experience was necessary for wholeness, and he saw dreams conveying very important insight into our spiritual journey toward God. His paradigms for interpreting dreams are very helpful because they give scientific data to help in recognizing the meaning of the dream components. We will draw on many of his discoveries, clarifying the content of specific parts of the dreamscape.

The People Paradigm: Meet the Rest of the Cast

Acknowledging these insights from earlier in the century, we have developed a unique paradigm for interpretation. Robert Wise has found a more colorful method, the "People Paradigm," for making sense out of the pieces of the dream. You've already been introduced to your movie-producer friend. Following the same cues, we will describe how many dream functions operate by describing the world of the mind as if it were populated with little people performing the mental processes that make us function.

At this point we are describing the subjective type of dream, revealing the unknown aspects of our personalities. Later, the objective variety of dream will be explored for insights about our relationship to the environment around us. In addition, archetypal dreams will be explored. However, for the moment we start with the important subjective dream to help us become whole, integrated human beings.

Remember, a paradigm is only an attempt to describe abstract experience in concrete terms so we will more accurately understand and know how to use our insights. The People Paradigm is a practical, straightforward model for understanding the components in the dream. Don't worry that your local brain surgeon wouldn't talk in these terms; he still dreams the same way with the help of the same little friends you're about to meet. Sit back and enjoy the entire cast used to make your nightly stage shows.

The first step is to understand what created a need for dreams. Dreams emerge as an attempt to put us in touch with a displaced realm in our inner world. Displacement begins in childhood as our personalities take shape.

We are born emotionally and mentally whole but quickly discover that certain personal aspects of who we are aren't acceptable to the parental figures who guarantee our security. Their facial responses, words, scoldings, anger, and displeasure tell us some components of our personalities must go. But memories don't disappear. Virtually every major ingredient in our experience is carefully preserved. The result has been the division of the world into acceptable and unacceptable thoughts, feelings, memories, and perceptions. In short order we constructed the up-front world of conscious experiences and a back room filled with the forbidden. However, in the secret room the unacceptable portions are stored for future reference. Our personalities develop a conscious and an unconscious realm. For our purposes we will call the suppressed world "the Wilderness."

The Wilderness becomes like the dark side of the moon. Unseen, it still supports and holds together the personality. Yesterday's rejected ideas, values, and experiences are forced to wander through these hinterlands like pariahs. Like lost little people, they want a reprieve from their exile. Their pressure creates the dream.

Our task is to make our abstract past experiences as concrete as possible so we can work with their meaning. We've found thinking of them as "lost little people" creates understanding of how our emotions, thoughts, and whims affect our perceptions of reality. Obviously, we don't mean for you to take us literally. We're not talking about spirit guides, actual entities, or physiological structures crawling around in our heads.

During early childhood, Robert Wise became fascinated with the human body's workings and wanted his grandmother to explain how digestion, blood flow, tiredness, speech, and thinking occurred.

"Well, Robert," Grandmother Wise began, "let's look around the house and see how we keep things running."

She opened the closet containing the panels of electrical fuses and demonstrated how electricity operated. She went downstairs and explained the floor furnace's operation. Next, she stopped by the washing machine and gave a quick lecture on what made it tick, then extended the lesson to include plumbing and drains.

"Son," she instructed, "why don't you think of your body as being like our house? Think of little people running around inside you, throwing switches, turning on your bloodstream just like we open a water tap, and keeping everything going. When you drift off to sleep, these little people throw the power switch to let you shut down. Because you're fatigued, someone operates the washing machine to clean the tiredness out of your blood, and when you awake you're filled with energy. The little people keep you fit!"

Robert didn't really believe he had a hidden race of leprechauns living just under his skin, but he did have a vivid model for getting in touch with what was going on in his body. Going to sleep made sense. Tiredness meant, "Time to turn on the washing machine." Abstract functions that were too complex for a five-year-old now made sense!

In a similar way, you don't have the time to get a college degree explaining how the intricacies of the mind operate. You just want to get down to business understanding your dreams.

The People Paradigm is Robert Wise's way of putting handles on mental abstractions. From this point forward, many of the functions of the unconscious mind will be described by giving personality to inner urges and needs. We're going to personify abstract components of our emotional life.

Messages from the Work Crew

The Wilderness provides a very important vantage point. Our misplaced friends who reside there have their own unique and highly perceptive perspectives. They may even have a wisdom that exceeds what we thought we possessed. When allowed to speak, these expatriates tell us profound truths about difficult situations we are currently facing. If nothing else, these little friends enable us to stand back and objectively view our behavior. In the shadowlands of their world, they generally see things much more clearly than we do in the light of day. The actors in the movie speak by dressing up and producing a movie. They create dreams as their vehicle of communication. Each night they shout their insights to us, trying to help us avoid mistakes and keep us from going down dead-end streets. They turn the windmills of our minds.

The need for integration provides the energy motivating our little helpers. Each of us has a God-given drive toward wholeness. Like Keebler cookie elves, the inner mechanisms insist on quality control. In fact, if you ignore their messages the dispatches will come roaring back in some other way such as depression or angry outbursts. Our dreams are highly significant processes, working to restore the unity the Holy Spirit brings to our personalities.

The Doorkeeper

You ask, "Why can't we simply tear down the wall separating us from the Wilderness? Once we recognize the existence of the place, why can't we just go in?" Sorry. The Doorkeeper is a fierce, unrelenting guard. You need to know about his function.

Depth psychology calls the Doorkeeper "the ego." Unfortunately, in popular usage *ego* is used as an adjective rather than a noun. Often the word becomes a description of self-centeredness or self-serving personality characteristics. Since the term is used in such a wide and confusing range of meanings, we're going to use the Doorkeeper label instead.

The Doorkeeper is actually the center of consciousness. He keeps us sane, ordered, and centered in reality. When overwhelming experiences come pouring in, the Doorkeeper coordinates our thoughts, feelings, and intentions. The Doorkeeper's job is to push out of view whatever is too painful, frightening, or threatening for us to face.

Without the strength of the Doorkeeper we would be overwhelmed by aspects of life beyond our management. A strong ego, or Doorkeeper, is vital to our well-being. If the Doorkeeper gets sick, we become mentally ill.

We can envision the Doorkeeper sitting behind a large computer positioned in the center of our nervous system, cataloging the events happening to us. He is coordinating their effects with the proper responses. His job is to make sure we come off as socially appropriate. When he does his job well, we look suave and competent. When circumstances overwhelm the Doorkeeper, he becomes a frazzled, disoriented administrator who leaves us appearing nervous, edgy, and defensive.

Unfortunately, the Doorkeeper has a fundamental problem of not being able to trust anything. Nothing affects his performance like fear, rejection, and shame. When these emotions pour in, he pushes the panic button and flushes everything downstairs to the Wilderness. The threatening material is no longer accessible until the Doorkeeper decides it is safe to take a peek. The clinical name for this process is *denial*. Usually counseling is required to put us in touch with the fact that the Doorkeeper has been playing a game with us all of our lives.

Dreams are possible because the Doorkeeper needs sleep. When we doze off, he also slumbers away, leaving the door unguarded. Our loss of consciousness allows the people in the Wilderness to open the denial barriers. Dreams surge forth from the unguarded moments.

The content of subjective dreams seems to be about something "you" are doing. What you seem to be doing in the dream is actually a picture of the inner drama going on between the Doorkeeper and the suppressed aspect of your past. Think of the "you" in your dreams as the conscious, all-seeing eye of the Doorkeeper, trying to survey every aspect of your world. Perhaps, it would be more helpful in diagramming your dreams if you wrote the "I" as "I=Eye."

Once you see the difference between the "I=Eye" and who you are as a human being, you will see why at important times you have been divided against yourself. Perhaps you've had moments when you felt your behavior was more a caricature than an accurate representation of your true self. The Doorkeeper can so completely control us that we literally lose our soul without knowing what's happened.

The Doorkeeper's tightfisted control can cause many people to become poor examples of the faith they profess. For some, Christianity is just another suit of clothes the Doorkeeper wears. If so, they only wear a spiritual cloak over the dirty shirt they need to change. Our dreams give us the lowdown on what the Doorkeeper is up to. Once the dream is read, you have a way to shut down the masquerade.

The Self

And what do we find after the party's over? In those moments when we are truly whole, what's there? *The Self.*

As we mature, grow, integrate, and become whole, the Doorkeeper is less able to control our perception of reality. The real "us" comes to the fore. Once we accept in ourselves the good and the bad, the strong and the weak, the rational and the feeling, the male and the female, the conscious and the unconscious, we develop oneness of being. This is the new identity we call the Self.

The Self emerges as we grow to understand our personal uniqueness. We recognize how we are different from parents, friends, peers, social groups, or political entities. Our sense of identity is becoming more accurate, appropriate, and clear. We begin to identify our place in the universe. There is a wonderful sense of reconciliation with our world.

Because every human being has an inner drive toward wholeness, the Doorkeeper is not allowed to impede forward progress forever. Like a butterfly emerging from a cocoon, the Self pushes and pulls until completion is accomplished. In addition, the Holy Spirit works to enable the Self to work past denial and deceit in a continual process of spiritual and emotional development. Our dreams give us status reports on the state of progress.

The Self appears in many forms. Often the dream speaks of the whole person by offering us the symbol of a house or a car. We may dream of a childhood house or a house under attack. The appearance of the house can tell us how we see ourselves. The rooms in the house reflect compartments in our lives. (For example, the kitchen may be a place of nurture.) We can look at our dream car and have a sense of the state of the Self. The driver of our car tells us volumes about who and what is controlling our lives. The people riding in the car with us offer clues to what may have invaded our lives. A child or an animal can embody the Self. The Self symbol is one of the most important forms we learn to identify.

The Alter-Gender

Men dream about women; women dream about men. Who are these symbolic members of the opposite sex appearing in our dream? Like the idea of an alter ego, these people are often our Alter-Genders.

Depth psychology, which has evolved from the work of Carl Jung, perceptively recognized men as having a feminine side and women as having a masculine dimension. These complementary aspects of our personalities are important for balance and emotional health. Brave, dominating men need the capacity for feelings of tenderness and compassion. Gentle, kind women will be called upon to assert themselves and take leadership. As these forces of both caring and aggressiveness arise in men and women, they shape our perceptions and responses.

The movie *Junior* offers a bizarre but insightful illustration of getting in touch with Alter-Gender. The comedy is the story of a cold, hard scientist who ends up the object of his own experiments. Arnold Schwarzenegger becomes pregnant! As the baby develops, the biological process puts him in touch with the much-needed feminine qualities of gentleness and maternal concern. While the movie sounds rather silly, Arnold's restored vulnerability certainly makes a valuable point.

If men deny the feminine side of their personalities, they turn into Ebenezer Scrooges and become mean-spirited. In our society men generally don't allow the deep-feeling component of their lives to have free rein. The hard-nosed businessman, the tyrannical prosecuting attorney, and the overbearing husband are the result of a loss of feminine influence on the personality.

Charles Dickens's immortal classic, *A Christmas Carol,* is the story of the resurrection of a man's feminine side. Through Scrooge's powerful dream, he discovers how compassion has been strangled out of his life. Put in dream language, the female Alter-Gender is resurrected as the crusty old man stands by his own grave and realizes that cold-heartedness has already made him a dead man. Remorse for his mistakes allows Ebenezer's long-dormant feminine side to come back to life.

On the other hand, women struggle with becoming dominated and overpowered by their masculine sides. Men don't pay enough attention to their Alter-Genders; women give too much credence to theirs. When her masculine side overwhelms and dominates a woman, she becomes a highly opinionated and domineering person who tends to be critical and make disparaging remarks about friends, associates, and family. The Alter-Gender–dominated woman is argumentative and dogmatic. While the masculine component will help women become brave and assertive, too much male force in the personality will produce women who crave power and are overly controlling.

In just this way, extreme feminists have often hurt the cause of women's rights. The bra-burning, unisex style, and the coarse talk of the extremist often betray an ego dominated and controlled by the masculine side. Such women cannot see their crusade against injustice has caused an imbalance in their own psyches.

How do we recognize the problem? The Alter-Gender person shows up in our dreams as a person of the opposite sex. Men will dream about interacting with women who are the composite of their feminine side. In turn, the men in women's dreams will generally embody the content of their masculine side.

Jim, one of Paul Meier's clients, had a clear Alter-Gender dream that served as a wake-up call. During this time, he often found himself in conflict with a woman in the church. Every time they were together, the woman made him bristle. She was pushy, catty, and generally belligerent. Ann showed up in his dream passing out lemons to everyone in sight. As he analyzed the dream, Jim realized the image was right on target. Ann left a sour taste in everyone's mouth . . . at least, in his.

Then Jim asked the jackpot question: Why was Ann showing up in his dreams? Of all people, he certainly wasn't attracted to her! Slowly, the cold realization settled! What he so bitterly disliked in the woman was a projection of something operating in his own personality. The dream warned of the same lack of feeling in him when he was dealing with other people. Ann represented a negative Alter-Gender image. Jim needed to reassess the same qualities in himself he found in Ann. She acted without concern for other people's feelings, and sometimes so did Jim!

The Alter-Gender figure shows up in dreams to make us aware that we are either over-functioning or under-functioning emotionally. Usually this symbol is calling attention to behavior we have ignored.

Many times people are shocked by sexual episodes in their dreams. We automatically jump to the conclusion that something immoral is brewing between us and the other person. Ninety percent of the time this assumption is totally the wrong conclusion. Actually, we are trying to come to terms with the Alter-Gender role! Because this subject is worthy of much more detailed consideration, we will look at these sexual dreams in much greater detail in a later chapter.

Many relationship problems begin when the Alter-Gender component in our personalities gets out of whack. Like a tyrannical dorm mother turning a college dormitory into an abysmal place to live, our personalities sour when possessed by a runaway Alter-Gender. If men ignore their feminine sides, they will be subject to depressive moods or uncontrollable emotional outbursts. They may become sloppy with sentiment or turn maudlin or morose. Their fantasy lives send them on mental wild-goose chases.

Women have a different but equally disruptive set of problems. An overly critical masculine Alter-Gender makes a woman feel inferior, unworthy, or judged. If one's conscience is captured by muscle-flexing domination, the result will be unrelenting guilt about everything. On the other hand, when the Doorkeeper is overpowered by the masculine function, the woman becomes a crusading feminist with the compassion of a gladiator. Imbalance in either direction is highly destructive.

To help you develop a sense of the Alter-Gender, we've compiled a list of negative masculine and feminine traits. When a character of the opposite sex shows up with these qualities, you've got a fairly good clue about why the dream is trying to get your attention.

Negative masculine qualities. These adjectives can be used to describe negative masculine qualities: aggressive, domineering, loud, competitive, rude, brutal, boorish, cruel, tough, ruthless, lustful, jealous, proud, arrogant, smug, sarcastic, cold, stubborn, patronizing, argumentative, critical, shrewd, suspicious, and impersonal.

Negative feminine qualities. These adjectives can be used to describe negative feminine qualities: weak, passive, slavish, self-indulgent, weepy, fragile, wishy-washy, seductive, coy, flirtatious, fickle, vain, extravagant, chatterbox, silly, sentimental, naive, moody, petty, catty, prudish, manipulative, possessive, complaining, nagging, pouting, smothering, and spiteful.

Have you seen any of these folks walking through your dreams? Get to know them, and they'll help you refrain from reproducing their behavior the next day. Remember, awareness is only the beginning of change. We must wrestle with the negative components in personality until our best side prevails.

Not all men and women in our dreams will be Alter-Gender representations. Sometimes they will be wisdom figures, real-life people, or parents. We may see multiple personalities of the opposite sex that have multiple meanings. However, when the opposite sex appears in your dreams, a good starting point for investigation is this interpretation of the person.

Masculine and feminine components are formed from the collective results of early experiences with fathers and mothers. Our ideal man or woman is fundamentally a product of the earliest perceptions of our parents. When anyone bearing this image walks into our lives, we are physically drawn to them. If we meet their expectation of the model Alter-Gender, the sky lights up with fireworks, hearts nearly explode, and it's love at first sight! Often people stumble into affairs because they are unaware of the dynamics of this inner magnetism. However, if they listened to their dreams, the warning would be there.

The Shadow

This chapter will not exhaust the possibilities of all the images in our dreams. However, one other figure must be identified for the moment. When we dream of persons of the same sex, we often meet the shadow side of the Wilderness, particularly if the figure is inferior or has unpleasant qualities.

Like the old radio character Lamont Cranston, the Shadow knows the most secret of secret truths about us. We don't like to acknowledge our inferior side. However, as the Doorkeeper locks unacceptable traits from our eyes, the residue forms a composite that turns into our Shadow. Generally people protest the existence of such a dimension, but their spouses can exactly describe the content of their unseen side. For other clues about the shape and form of this ethereal part of you, consider the characteristics you really dislike in another person. What we project onto others arises out of our Shadow side.

The Shadow contains our primitive and uncivilized urges. The book *Dr. Jekyll and Mr. Hyde* describes a very cultured man overpowered by his bestial hidden nature. The movie *Schindler's List* depicts the same instinctual urges erupting in violent passion. In each story, the main characters did not have an acceptable way to live with their dark sides and were overwhelmed by the Shadow's power. Repression of the Shadow's existence often results in moral explosions that wreck people's lives. On the other hand, failure to recognize the Shadow produces both hypocrisy and intolerance for which church people are often noted, unfortunately.

Moral courage and humility are required to face up to the content of the Shadow lurking in the Wilderness. But here's the surprise: Sifting through the "garbage" leads to a wonderful discovery. What seemed so repugnant generally turns out to be pure gold!

Many of our most important qualities arise out of primitive forces waiting to be tamed and harnessed. Lust can become holy passion; violent anger turns into righteous indignation. Suffering develops the seedbed from which creativity springs and blossoms. When we cease to be strangers to ourselves, we allow redemption to penetrate our every facade. Our dreams provide the quickest and most effective way of hearing the Shadow's message and unraveling the mysteries of our dark side.

Using the People Paradigm: Your Assignment

Now that we are on a first-name basis with many of the little people running around in our heads, we have a clearer idea of what the movie director works with as well as the content spinning out from the windmills of our mind. Let's go back to the beginning of this chapter and see if we can help Tom find the clues needed to make sense out of his dream.

But before we begin, let us make one thing clear: No one can tell another person what his or her dreams mean. Attempts at authoritative interpretation are always the mark of the amateur or the quack. In the same way, books pronouncing the exact meaning of all dream symbols are as valueless as a horoscope. However, we can ask insightful questions leading people to make their own discoveries. Therefore, dream work is more a matter of intelligent observation than dogmatic assertion. In Tom's case, the job was to help him answer his own questions.

Tom was stuck. His life needed a radical change, but he was afraid to go forward. His inability to understand his issues turned into depression and despair. Although Tom was a thoroughly good and moral person, his self-doubts held him with the vise-like grip of a guilty conscience. He couldn't understand why.

Before you read further, take a piece of paper and diagram Tom's dream as you learned to do in previous chapters. Break down the dream into the four major segments and note what's in the cast of characters and symbols. Then, using what you've learned in this chapter, see what you can identify and label using the People Paradigm.

No fair peeking! You will learn only to the degree you practice. Start now.

Here's one way you might diagram the dream:

Setting

I

making a trip

truck

avoiding repairs

still start the trip

Problem

find a service station

half in/half out

tools

hesitant to get permission

start work to save money

garage owner friendly

Because

cost is $51

feel overcharged

can't decide to pay

Solution

locust on window

Scripture passage

opera *Parsifal*

Now, go over your outline before you start exploring the symbols. Do you notice the Doorkeeper needs to leave town and find a new place to live? It's time to move on. But there's a problem! The ole ego isn't sure the vehicle for transportation can make it.

What did you make of the truck? Remind you of anything? Sure. The truck, like the car, is a symbol of the Self. Tom's self isn't a sporty convertible or even a practical family car. The best image

Tom can muster of himself is an old, beat-up, worn-out truck. This symbol tells us volumes about why Tom has such severe self-doubts.

Tom can't get on with his life because the "Doorkeeper" won't let him make up his mind about getting his view of himself fixed. He keeps vacillating between fully confronting himself and his issues or simply putting Band-Aids on his problems. Tom is sabotaged internally even though he recognizes that staying in his problem is very costly.

What did you make of the service station? The fact that Tom is half in and half out of the building? Did you guess that the place where Tom was in therapy might be the garage? Obviously Tom is only "half into" his therapy. He's not entirely committed to change. In fact, for three years he has wandered in a barren, emotional no-man's-land. Therein lies both the issue in the problem segment of the dream and in everyday life!

Tom's life sounds like a farmer's wheat crop after locusts have ravaged the fields. *Locusts?* Have we seen that word somewhere before?

The image of Tom's sister comes next. You probably want to ask him some questions about his relationship with his sister to determine what she symbolizes in the dream. Perhaps she could be an Alter-Gender figure. She might even have possibilities as a new Self symbol. Either way, a biblical passage suggests God will restore what Tom lost over the past three years. On a hunch we might guess that the feminine, feeling side of Tom's life is offering him a message of hope. He can quit being a victim of the past and perceived failures. In fact, God will help him really get a life if he will "give up the truck."

As this line of questions was being pursued, Tom was suddenly filled with insight. He realized how much he was afraid of failure. His "I=Eye" was in a state of confusion trying to avoid confrontation with his internal misgivings. His "I=Eye" was afraid to pay the price for change and was subverting the therapy process. Tom realized he had the capacity to take control of his life. He wasn't going to be held captive by fear!

Little discussion was needed to make sense out of the prelude to *Parsifal*. Tom loved classical music and knew the story. The opera is the saga of a spiritual quest for the Holy Grail as a symbol for personal fulfillment. In fact, the complete saga of *Parsifal, the Fisher King, and the Grail* is a remarkable parallel to Tom's need to heal childhood wounds and fully become his own person. The prelude was Tom's call to his own crusade for holy wholeness.

In one hour of dream work, Tom got the stalled truck out of the garage and on its way to the junkyard. As a statement of his changed attitude, Tom traded in the truck for a new car the next weekend. He was a new man.

Chapter 6

THE TUNNEL TO
YOUR SOUL
More Pieces to the Puzzle

Song to My Other Self

Over the years I have caught glimpses of you
in the mirror, wicked;
in a sudden stridency in my own voice, have
heard you mock me; . . .
You are there, lurking under every kind act I do,
ready to defeat me. . . .
I have looked for you with new eyes
opened to your tricks, but more,
opened to your rootedness in life
Come, I open my arms to you also,
*   once-dreadstranger.*
Come, as a friend I would welcome you. . .
Thus I would disarm you.
For I have recently learned,
learned looking straight in your eyes;
The holiness of God is everywhere.
ELSIE LANDSTROM, *INWARD LIGHT*, NO. 67

D r. Meier, please help me!" the nurse began the session. "I've had a rather disturbing dream."

"I'll do my best," Paul answered. "Just tell me your experience, Sally."

"In my dream I was in charge of a dialysis unit, and I was training a new nurse without using the very complex rule book. I awoke feeling quite frustrated. I had an impression that my life was out of control because the trainee couldn't live up to all the rules she was supposed to keep."

In fact, Sally *was* the head nurse in a dialysis unit at a local hospital. Paul quickly recognized the objective quality in her dream. A recent victim of the empty-nest syndrome, Sally's family world was radically changing, and during this time her favorite uncle had died. In fact, her life was far from under control. In addition, Sally's perfectionism drove her to never miss a detail at home or on the job. Consequently, she had evolved quite naturally to the top position of responsibility in the dialysis unit. Her dream expressed the nurse's frustration in trying to do *everything* right!

Paul didn't have to look far for the implications because the dream was set in Sally's place of work. The nurse needed to recognize how her blind ambition was making her life miserable.

Here's another dream of a different type. See if you notice the difference.

"Dr. Wise," Mae began, "I've had the most wonderful dream." Tears came to her eyes. "But the whole experience has left me feeling bitter and empty. I just don't understand."

Mae began telling the dream story of her long-deceased brother's return to life. A telegram reported George's death was nothing more than a fabrication. The army had shipped an expensive sealed casket to deceive the family. At the dream funeral, Mae couldn't look into the casket because it was sealed. While this was going on the military was hiding George at another location. Mae was elated and overjoyed that her brother could return to her. He had been an extremely important part of her life. However, when Mae awoke she was quite unhappy and resentful. In contrast to what she might have expected, the dream had left her feeling angry. Mae was quite confused by the symbols and didn't know how to interpret the experience.

"What actually happened at your brother's real funeral?" Robert asked. "After the army returned your brother's body did you look in the casket?"

"No," Mae answered slowly. "The casket was sealed, and no one ever knew for sure who was inside."

"Did the lack of identification trouble you?"

"Absolutely," Mae shot back.

As they discussed her memories of the long-past experience, Mae once more became aware of how much she had depended on her brother. She resented his not being around to talk with her. Slowly, she began to see the dream was telling her how much she *wanted* to keep George alive. Mae was preserving her brother's existence in the unconscious Wilderness of her mind.

The dream forced Mae to face up to a very significant issue. Deep down inside her psyche, Mae was trying to wrap reality around an illusion. The hope of resurrecting her brother was the center of a diluted hope. In effect, Mae had a brother complex. There couldn't be wholeness until she "buried" her brother.

Because Robert knew Mae wasn't facing her emotional needs directly, he asked her if she felt any sorrow at the funeral. To her amazement, Mae realized she had never grieved for her brother; she had not shed one tear from the moment she had heard of his death. Gradually, the larger picture came into focus. Mae was a victim of her own unresolved grief. Her personal need of an older brother to lean on had kept a delusion alive.

To allow the dream message to do its work, Robert suggested that Mae find something that was an important memento of her brother. She immediately thought of his large picture in the center of her bedroom wall. Robert instructed Mae to take the picture down, wrap it, and prepare it for burial. She was going to reconstruct the funeral, and this time she would grieve. As the wrapped picture was literally buried in the backyard, Mae was to see herself standing before an open casket, looking at George and truly saying good-bye to her brother.

Mae went home, removed the picture, and began preparing the portrait as if it were a person being laid in his casket. As strange as the instructions might sound, once Mae completed the symbolic committal, the effects of her unresolved grief disappeared. She stopped the wishful thinking that he might return. Most important, she let go of her brother's emotional hold on her life. Mae was able to go on alone without the need of an old dependency on her brother.

See a difference in the dreams yet? Mae's dream was subjective while Sally's was objective.

Objective and Subjective Dreams

The previous chapters have given us a feel for the symbolic nature of dreams and offered clues for how to pull the symbols apart to read them. But dreams are not all the same kind. Now we will look more deeply into the type, or form, of the dream experience.

Objective Dreams

Sally's dream was related to what was happening in her *immediate environment*. The nurse was dreaming about her actual place of work. Real events and their influence on the nurse were the heart of the matter. Such dreams can appropriately be called objective.

However, Mae's dream was definitely subjective. The issues were concerned with hidden and forgotten dimensions of Mae's past pain. She was called to explore the Wilderness, looking behind the shadowy shapes of her past.

Caution! Some symbols are just too obtuse to understand, and some dreams will never be deciphered. Don't worry if some dreamscapes can't be fathomed. We will have plenty to work on with the material we do grasp. If you can't make any sense out of a particular dream, don't worry. Important messages will come back in other forms.

Generally, it's best to begin by assuming the dream is objective, attempting to tell us something that is literally true. When the dream coincides with real places, people, and events we are encountering immediately in everyday life, we have a strong clue that the communiqué is about a current situation.

The objective dream doesn't tend to have the same depth of symbolic meaning found in subjective dreams. You quickly get the sense of watching a movie of a contemporary situation. The setting and the structure correspond to your immediate location.

For example, a nun dreamed of flying above the heads of her school students in their classroom. She was truly the "flying nun." At first the dream was baffling, as everything about the scene seemed exactly as would have been true of her in the classroom except that she was zooming around like a bird.

The sister knew enough about dream work to avoid the mistake of assuming the dream was only rehashing something that had occurred the day before. If a dream picks up on last night's TV program or the last conversation you had, etc., it's because you've missed an important notice those experiences can convey to you.

As the nun wrestled with the motif of "flying above their heads," the information became clear. She was teaching "over their heads"! She wasn't communicating on her students' level. The dream helped change her style of teaching, and dramatic improvement followed in the classroom.

Once you get the basic message of an objective dream you've got the point!

When Robert Wise's youngest son Tate was six weeks old, the baby had an extremely serious and life-threatening intestinal problem. Unless the obstruction in his bile duct could be removed, Tate would quickly die. Robert was completely overwhelmed as no child in his area had ever survived such surgery. The night before the operation Robert stayed at the hospital with Tate, weeping through the night, for he was sure the tiny infant could not survive the surgery. He weighed less than six pounds!

The next morning Robert's wife arrived in an unusually cheerful state of mind for such a tragic moment. During the night she had dreamed the surgeon repaired the problem, and she described the procedure in detail. Since neither of them knew anything about medicine or what lay ahead, Robert assumed she had simply flipped out; he discounted her story.

Hours later an excited surgeon hurried into the waiting room. The operation had gone far better than his wildest expectations. As he described the procedure, Robert nearly fell out of his chair. His wife had described the operation in almost the same, identical words just a few hours earlier. God had graciously given them comfort through this objective dream.

Subjective Dreams

Only after we have explored and exhausted the possibility of an objective dream do we consider the possibility of a subjective dream context. This form takes us far below the surface of everyday life into the realm controlled by our old nemesis, the Doorkeeper. Because dreams tell us something we haven't consciously recognized, don't be surprised at the mysterious quality, which can be quite confounding. In fact, if you think you see the meaning immediately, you probably have missed the message. Common forms may be used to get us to see an uncommon twist in their meaning.

Subjective dreams often push us to find new meaning from our past experiences, helping bring all the issues in our lives toward wholeness and into relationship with God. Our dreams portray the fact that we are incurably religious. The heavenly Father has created us with an impulse that can only be satisfied in relationship to Himself. Dreams spur us on to expose every experience to heavenly light.

Sometimes our dreams produce catharsis, which heals the brokenness of the past. We are literally being led to "confess" our sins, our transgressions, and our debts from yesterday. Dream interpretation is generally not complete until we bring repressed needs into a fresh encounter with the Holy Spirit. At such times our dreams are the windows to our soul.

Spectacular Dreams

And what about those overwhelming occasions when unicorns romp through the dream, fairies dance on the bedspread, overpowering images loom up before us, strange creatures appear, or awesome events happen? When people have numinous experiences of God they always feel totally overcome by the dream. We will call such dreams "spectaculars."

Archetypal dreams put us in touch with great power for change. *Archetype* is a word for the original pattern or form of a power, a truth, an emotion, a way of life, or an instinct embodied in people, animals, structures, and images. Archetypes are symbols that have extraordinary power to mold and shape our behavior. These shapes remold lives into their image.

For example, kids with long hair, sandals, shredded blue jeans, and drug habits may be gripped by the hippie archetype. Their fathers, dressed in the latest Gucci shoes, designer tie, and double-breasted suit, may be equally possessed by the executive archetype.

These basic forms exert such great power they can even take over our lives. The Jim Joneses and David Koreshes are frightening examples of what happens when religious people are swallowed by the messiah archetype. Our dreams will tell us when we are living out a double, a counterpart that isn't the real us. By the same token, such dreams may make us aware of great forces that are or can impact, reshape, and empower our lives.

For many people an American flag is an archetype of patriotism. A flag evokes love of country; emotion surges within us as we see it snapping in the wind. A wedding ring is an archetype of love and fidelity. After a death or divorce, the removal of the ring from the finger causes excruciating pain. The cross, a Christian archetype, causes people to remember the death of Jesus for their sin. Consequently, crosses on buildings automatically tell us volumes about what can be expected inside. When similar symbols are dominant factors in dreams, the archetypes are being evoked. Each form has a significant power to motivate us.

The power of an archetype can be compared to the weather. Wind, rain, cold, and storms make us feel everything from depressed to fearful to happy. The weather report shapes our expectations of the day. Free will and our ability to make decisions are not removed or overwhelmed by what's blowing outside, yet we feel the influence of the temperature and the overcast skies. Archetypes are like storms blowing in from the Wilderness.

The highly significant capacity of an archetype to shape our behavior can be further clarified by observing how children and teenagers are affected by models they see on television or in the movies. Power Rangers, Barney, Ninja Turtles, Barbie, Rocky, Roy Rogers, and rock stars such as Kiss, Madonna, etc., have costumes, behavior, and individual characteristics that are easily emulated. Kids dress and act like these characters. They cut their hair or even paint their faces to appear to be like their hero or heroine. Of course, the fad eventually passes, but for a time their imagination is captured. These *outer* images impact young people through what they see.

On the other hand, the archetype is an *inner* image that affects far more than imagination. Thinking, ideals, and values are under the strongest influence of their force. More than cartoon image, the archetype summarizes and collects primal and primitive powers. The warrior, crusader, mother, seductress, monster, priest, Amazon character, etc., are larger-than-life types. Often, a contemporary type actually reflects a more universal and ancient image. For example, the hippie is a recent caricature of the ancient rebel type. The man in the expensive business suit who drives a Rolls Royce and expects special treatment at the country club may be acting out a modern version of king. The appearance of such forms and shapes creates spectacular dreams.

Robert Wise has never known anyone with the frequency and magnitude of spectacular dreams that his son, Tate, enjoys. After surviving the risky surgery when he was just six weeks old, Tate was plunged into another terribly frightful medical experience at age six. Possibly such early pain opened a depth in his soul that gave him an unusual touch with the archetypal depths in his unconscious mind.

When he was a junior in high school, Tate came to Robert with a staggering dream. He was in first-century Jerusalem, being swept along with a crowd of people marching into the courtyard of the Antonia fortress where Pontius Pilate was standing on a high balcony. Tate felt himself jostled by the angry crowd crying out for an execution. Suddenly soldiers appeared with a prisoner bound in chains. The first human being in all history staggered up beside the Roman magistrate. Adam was the prisoner!

The crowd cried out, "Crucify him. Crucify Adam for what he has done to us!"

Pilate loosened the chains binding Adam and declared to the mob, "No! I have been here once before. I will not make the same mistake twice. Release the man!"

Adam was set free.

Obviously, such a dream is beyond either an objective or subjective category. Spectacular dreams touch the eternal and force us to recognize we have encountered transcendent truth.

To understand such encounters we often have to look for historical or ancient meanings of the symbols. Remember the biblical story of Joseph in Egypt? For example, to understand Pharaoh's dream, we must ask what cows meant in ancient Egypt. If I dream of pyramids or see chariots of fire descending, I must turn to the larger, more universal implications of these images.

Many of the dreams in the Bible are of this higher order. For example, Daniel's dream of four beasts is obviously of a higher order. The archetypes are overpowering: a lion with the wings of an eagle, a flesh-eating bear, a four-winged leopard with four heads, and finally, a horrible creature with iron teeth and ten horns.[1]

King Nebuchadnezzar's dream of a great tree is similar. After being shown a timber reaching into the heavens, the king heard the command to cut it down and leave the stump bound with iron. The scene was followed with glimpses of a man being turned into a beast. Frightening consequences followed when Nebuchadnezzar ignored the warning in the dream and became psychotic.[2]

Joseph's interpretation of the pharaoh's dream images of seven lean and seven fat cows, signifying years of plenty and famine, was clearly archetypal. Cattle were sacred symbols in Egypt and conveyed messages about prosperity.[3]

At Bethel, Jacob dreamed of a magnificent ladder reaching from earth to heaven. The place of God's dwelling had been found. The sight of angels going up and down the ladder assured Jacob of God's blessing.[4]

While we haven't exhausted the subject, we can recognize the

96

nature of these overpowering experiences that come with the force of storm waves crashing against a shoreline.

Sometimes personal and spectacular dreams blend elements of each together. When we *cannot* make immediate meaningful associations with the symbols or find any place in our experience where the dream content fits, chances are high we are in an archetypal dream. Hang on to your hat! A great experience is awaiting your interpretation.

The High Cost of Inflation

Let's shift gears and look at what happens when we are overpowered by archetypes. Common vernacular often inaccurately describes arrogant or pretentious people as having too much ego. As a matter of fact, one can't have too much ego, the vehicle that ensures stability. What we really mean is ego distortion, which is called inflation. The archetype has taken over and is twisting our self-perception.

Yes, inflation is more than an economic problem. In the world of business if the actual value of goods has been distorted and the price is too high, the entities are referred to as having inflated worth. We know a crash is coming because of over-evaluation. In the same way, when the Doorkeeper loses his perspective we have a serious personality-inflation problem. Disaster is ahead!

When personality-inflation occurs, everyday people are swallowed by over-evaluated images. (If you don't think so, just watch a political convention!) The archetypes in our spectacular dreams are highly instructive for personal stability. We need to know how our lives are affected by the power forces quite apart from the dream process.

Archetypes have the power to overpower our internal sense of direction and seduce us into identifying so completely with their form and content that our identity merges with their image. During the era of German national socialism, the swastika came to be an archetype of Aryan world supremacy. German citizens were so obsessed with the ideas of Adolf Hitler they lost all sense of proportion and believed they were invincible. Even as Germany's impending defeat in World War II was completely obvious, they refused to accept reality. Belief in secret weapons, Hitler's magic ability to lead, the impregnability of their borders—one bizarre idea after another was tenaciously held as bombs crashed down on their heads. Even today the swastika remains an alluring archetype to racist and hate mongers whose fears of their own personal weaknesses cause them to hunger for control over others.

In Miguel de Cervantes's moving story *Don Quixote,* we read of a person so overburdened with the cruelty of the world that he too closely identified with the knight archetype. The old man found a form into which he could pour his overwhelming burden of concern and turned into the slightly mad knight of the woeful countenance.

The first time Robert Wise saw the Broadway production of *The Man of La Mancha,* which is based on *Don Quixote,* he was amazed at the overpowering effect of the play. He stood to break into wild applause as the cast sang the deeply moving strains of "The Impossible Dream." Only in retrospect was he able to see the continuing influence of the archetypal pull toward dreaming the impossible dream, bearing the "unbearable sorrow," and righting the "unrightable wrong." He was ready to pick up a lance and ride!

Inflation is not nearly as easy to recognize in ourselves as we might think. It's easy to laugh at the foolishness of Don Quixote charging a windmill on horseback, but we see nothing humorous in our own attempts to leap tall buildings in a single bound. The momentary sense of omnipotence, the godlike ability, the complete mastery of others, etc., is intoxicating and highly exalting. We are so full of ourselves we are sure we have reached the apex of reality.

What we readily identify in others is completely obliterated in our own eyes. Tragically, the drunkenness of our personal deception is only leading us to a king-sized hangover that could destroy our lives.

The movie *Quiz Show* gives us a haunting picture of an inflated personal view that ruined the people caught up in the television–quiz-show scandals of the late fifties. We watch good men become corrupted by money and slowly seduced into thinking they are about to become national celebrities because of capacities they don't really have. If these men had known how to listen to their dreams, they might have been saved from a lifetime of disgrace.

Lawyers with vicious courtroom techniques believe there is no limit to their ability to destroy people . . . until their own treachery betrays them. Stockbrokers bending the security rules make millions because they believe they are smarter than the system . . . until they get caught. Politicians become so deluded with the lofty positions of office they consider themselves invincible . . . until they lose the next election. Each is an example of megalomania of the first order.

Our files contain the tragic story of a woman who was fascinated with the idea that she could change her role in life by intentionally claiming a new archetype for herself. She left the role of mother and wife behind to become seductress and warrior. As her obsession with the idea of the power of wolves took hold of her personality, this gentle creature metamorphosed into a treacherously dangerous woman who left great disaster in her wake. Her personality inflation destroyed her former self.

How often have you seen the quiet teenager turn hippie, the businessman in midlife crisis become a playboy, a bored housewife fiercely proclaim herself a liberationist, a person making some extra money suddenly act like he or she is wealthy? On and on the list goes as good people are destroyed by archetypal possession. Such persons generally began their journeys with flights of fancy into exotic daydreams. Next their dreams filled with chaotic forms and strange images. If the messages are ignored, they lose sight that their assumed ascent is actually a descent.

Paul Meier had a female patient with persistent dreams of being a great professional football player. This highly dominant woman was successful in the business world and felt no man was her equal. Finally, the aggressive woman came in for therapy. She dreamed of running as a back for the Dallas Cowboys until the opponents tackled her so hard she couldn't play anymore. Anyone miss the warning there?

Dreams work hard to tell us a disaster is ahead. We may dream images of airplanes crashing, cars going off cliffs, or drowning people not being rescued. Often after these dreams we will awake in a panic. Disturbing feelings will be our clue to pay careful attention to what is happening to us in our daily lives.

Recovering Our Souls

Our dreams' critical task is to make us completely and fully conscious, to know ourselves as we really are. Our dreams give us the most up-to-date information possible on the state of our minds. The point is to make sure we are not deceived into thinking our fragmented lives are actually whole. Dreams push us toward balance. The key issue is integrity.

The Bible identifies the similar results of the Holy Spirit's work in us, pushing us toward maturity and spiritual wisdom, freeing us of old injuries, and saving us from the mistakes of projecting our fears and inadequacies onto others. We do not misinterpret our own inner voices for the speech of God.

Your Assignment

Review the dreams you have collected to date and scan their content to identify how many are objective, subjective, and spectacular. Do you find you tilt toward subjective dreams? Objective dreamscapes? Do some dreams simply seem impossible to interpret? Get a sense of how you've experienced the various types.

If you have been working on your dreams and come up with interpretations, reconsider your conclusions. Is it possible there is additional meaning in these dreams pushing you on toward greater personal wholeness? Do your dreams contain any issues that could be blocking wholeness? Ask yourself about the spiritual implications of these dreams.

Maybe the Holy Spirit is at work!

Chapter 7

DISCERNMENT
The Other Side of Insight

For every war has its beginning in the heart and mind of man. The primary battle is with the inner enemy. Until a man has conquered in himself that which causes war, he contributes, consciously or unconsciously, to warfare in the world.
FRANCES G. WICKES, *THE INNER WORLD OF CHOICES*

A s we journey down the winding dream trail, important tools are being acquired to help you work
through your reveries. The People Paradigm provides a context for
interpretation and tuning in the messages sent from the Wilderness.
Now we need to develop further insight into reading dream messages. We have some important personal discoveries about discernment for you.

The Bible tells us, "The heart is deceitful above all things, and
desperately wicked; Who can know it?"[1] The unconscious mind is
not a reservoir of innocence waiting to pop up and shower us with
benevolence. Our continual tendencies toward aggression, projection, and repression are obvious evidence of the tilt. We must keep

tabs on the ever-elusive truth about our actual motivations. The development of an observing side is crucial for our well-being.

At the same time, there is a very significant push within each of us toward integrity and wholeness. While the conscience is one aspect of this urge, we have an even more basic need to keep faith with ourselves, with our souls. Dreams are an important part of this process.

Getting Our Act Together

The drive toward authenticity is often called "individuation." Our emerging true self needs to be set free from the domination of the Doorkeeper. Release is needed from the forces of the past trying to keep us locked into inadequate perceptions, denigrating experiences, and nagging phobias. Consequently, the unconscious mind pushes toward merger with consciousness. Dreams are not only an expression of this drive, but an attempt to accomplish the task. Therefore, one of the basic questions for dream interpretation is, "How is this experience attempting to bring greater unity to my life?"

An attractive young wife came to the Minirth Meier New Life Clinic seeking insight into a dream. Mary was a gentle soul, struggling to keep a family member from running over her.

"Dr. Meier," she began, "in my strange dream I was skiing with a very accepting girlfriend. I was wearing scanty shorts and having a great time being myself when the friend disappeared and my parents appeared. You won't believe what I did!"

Paul thought about Mary's usual passive-dependent responses and smiled. "I'll bet you acted in a surprisingly aggressive way."

"Exactly!" Mary exclaimed. "I picked up a shotgun and threatened the family if they came any closer. I even shot at the ceiling to scare them, firing until I ran out of shells. Finally, a dog and bird started telling me how my family felt so I could help them."

"Sounds like the dream says you need to take drastic action to get out from under their domination," Paul observed. "The symbols seem to be expressing how important it is for you to separate yourself from them."

Mary nodded her head and sighed. "I'm afraid so."

As a matter of fact, Mary had to work on learning how to stand up for herself while remaining a kind, sensitive person. If individuation was to occur, Mary had to detach herself from the influence and control of the authority figures in her life. The real Mary was stuck to the power of her parents. Individuation demanded distance!

As we approach midlife, our quest for independence and purpose becomes increasingly pressing. Regardless of previous success and accomplishment, people often become aware of a lack of fulfillment and meaningful direction. While the first half of life is preoccupied with activity and acquisition, the second half cannot be satisfying without firm bearing and clear meaning. Doing must eventually give way to being!

Our dreams may start asking hard questions about the frantic activity in our lives, particularly if the flash and fury signify nothing. One of Paul Meier's clients had such a dream at the point of entering midlife.

"The dream began with me getting off a bus to march with a band in a parade," he said. "Someone yelled, 'Hurry up. The parade is about to start.'

"I looked around and realized I was also supposed to march in a second band. But I didn't have the right uniform for the other band.

"I immediately hurried off to find the university where the other uniforms were kept. Unfortunately, there was no car, so I had to walk, which only increased the time problem. I went by the house where I had lived during college and stopped in. To my amazement, I found people there dressing in another style of uniform for a third band. They wanted me to join them. I realized it was impossible to fulfill all of these opportunities to march!

"At the time of the dream," the client adds, "I was out of town on a speaking engagement."

Are you beginning to get the picture?

"I reluctantly had to face what the dream was saying about my tendency to be a performer showing up for every parade going down the street. Even though I was always eager to make a super-human effort to fulfill all the obligations, demands, and opportunities put on me, the dream called attention to the limits of human possibility. You can't march in three bands at the same time! The dream suggested the necessity of boundaries on my activities. I needed to recognize that a parade made a poor substitute for real life. It was time to trade in a couple of uniforms. Discernment was needed."

But how do we get beyond the nonsense in our lives that masquerades as genuine value? Our dreams are of prime value in doing this. The content of each episode introduces the pressing issues. Having exciting dreams and playing with them is not enough. Dream work is far more significant than a few *"aha!"* insights. We must wrestle with the messengers as well as their messages until the insights are synthesized into the fabric of our very being. Only then can we achieve the individuation that is the prelude to wholeness. We have to become well acquainted with our cast of dream characters. We must get to know what makes the Doorkeeper tick and the Alter-Gender function, and we need to understand the content of our Shadow. In addition, we have to civilize the Wilderness. The better we understand these dimensions of ourselves, the more complete and whole our lives become.

We must put our discoveries into action as we observed Mae doing in Chapter 6 after her dream about her brother's funeral. The only way change would come was for Mae to act out an unfinished drama of grieving. By doing so she honored her dream's message.

We have no more choice about the pressure toward individuation than we do about being hungry if we haven't eaten. Failure to pay attention will only result in the perpetual unhappiness that is currently chronic in this society. The only option is whether we will allow our self-created roadblocks to stand or encourage our own natural tilt toward integration. Discernment is required.

Restless Until . . .

As early as the fourth century, Augustine of Hippo profoundly understood the problem of restlessness but described the issues in theological rather than psychological terms. "Our souls are restless," he wrote, "until they find rest in Thee."[2] Augustine recognized the issue of individuation is fundamentally religious. Even people who reject God can't avoid the spiritual problem. Until we find peace with God, we cannot find peace with ourselves. In this sense, dreams also have basic religious meanings and generally offer spiritual direction. Affirmation from numinous dreams can be life-changing.

After holding a weekend seminar on dream interpretation, we received a remarkable response from one of the participants. The day after the retreat, Amanda wrote this letter:

Dear Robert,

I had a remarkable dream this morning and knew I must tell you what happened. The whole adventure began with your instructing me on how to use a hot water heater, of all things. As I was listening, one of your sons was suddenly standing beside me with his arm around me and pressing his cheek next to mine. I began to realize this was a romantic overture. I felt love

*for your son, but knew he was much too young for me. I
thought about my age, my wrinkles, and how people would talk.
The scene shifted, and your son and I were seated on a
long bench. We were very close together, and he was holding me
tightly. Robert, you sat down at the other end of the bench and
people gathered. You immediately started instructing us, but you
kept looking at your son to make sure he approved and your
teaching was correct. You gave your son great authority to correct
anything which was wrong in your teaching. Finally you finished teaching, looked at your son, and asked, "Was that all
right?" Your son said nothing, but suddenly I realized the person holding me so closely was Jesus.*

*I awoke with the awestruck awareness I had experienced a
love beyond anything I had ever known. Jesus had come to me
as the lover of my soul and didn't care that I was too old, or
what anyone thought about me. I fell on my knees and thanked
Him with all my heart. What a way to begin the day, the week,
the rest of my life. I just had to share this experience with you.*

Amanda

Amanda experienced a powerful, integrating encounter
with the Holy Spirit. She received a special heavenly affirmation. As a result, Amanda could accept herself just as she was.
Such dreams draw no lines between the worlds of psychology
and theology.

When groups or individuals ignore spirituality, the inner religious dynamic does not shrivel and fade. To the contrary, the
energy redirects itself in often frighteningly destructive direc-
tions. People who vehemently proclaim atheism are sitting targets to be swept up in the fanaticism of Nazism, Communism, or
a similar "ism." They turn political systems into their religion.
Crusades, religious wars, witch-hunts, and inquisitions are the
by-products of a perverted need for the true God.

As the influences of secular humanism have grown in the public school system, superstition and devil worship have increased in American life. The corollary is not an accident. Failure to be spiritually whole is often reflected in twisted and morbid fascination with the occult. If modern education intended to free pupils from a need for spirituality and God, the experiment has been a devastating failure. Unfortunately, the educators have only set kids up for the worst forms of animism, pantheism, and civil religion.

Therefore, dream work flourishes within the Christian community. Scripture offers perimeters for testing insight and conclusions. Ritual and worship help frame our inner journeys with constructive boundaries down time-tested paths. We avoid the trap of treating spirituality as an independent entity. One of the errors of the so-called New Age thought is divorcing spiritual experience from genuine connection to God, as revealed in Jesus Christ. Time-tested creeds, confessions, catechisms, and doctrines help keep us balanced and away from dead-end aberrations.

On the other hand, dreams can help us accomplish a fundamental human task. We cannot be whole until our religious convictions are internalized and we encounter the life of God within us. When faith is only a veneer, we are hopelessly inadequate, both spiritually and emotionally. Dreams can be a vital part of our spiritual awakening. Interestingly enough, one of the major differences of opinion between Freud and Jung came at exactly this point. While Freud saw religion as a vestige of neuroticism, Jung believed any form of psychotherapy that ignored the patient's spiritual life was ultimately doomed to failure.

Jung wrote,

Too few people have experienced the divine image as the inner-most possession of their souls. Christ only meets them from without, never from within the soul; that is why dark paganism still reigns there, a paganism which, now in a form so blatant that it can no longer be denied and now in all too threadbare disguise, is swamping the world of so-called Christian culture.[3]

Our dreams can lead us to a new place of encounter with the Holy Spirit. Discernment is incomplete without working on and through the religious implications and dimensions of our dreams.

Discerning Questions

Here are five key questions to keep uppermost in mind as you pull the symbols apart:

1. Remember that the heart is deceitful and that you have a shadow side. Therefore, as you look at your dream ask yourself: *What am I hiding from myself?*

2. Remember that you are a fragmented person. Ask yourself: *How is this dream trying to bring greater unity to my life?*

3. Remember that you are often confused about what is authentic and real. Ask yourself: *How is this dream trying to reveal what is genuine?*

4. Remember that you tend to repress insight. Ask yourself: *How have I failed to pay attention to previous instruction and insight from my dreams?*

5. Remember that lingering and nagging restlessness is possibly a religious and spiritual problem. Ask yourself: *How is the Holy Spirit speaking to me?*

Each question will help expand your initial insights and frame your conclusions in the largest possible context.

Complex Problems

With these issues in mind, let's take a trip back into the Wilderness. We need to add another weapon to our arsenal of insights. Discernment demands that we take a long look at one of the strange phenomena operating in the outback, the complex.

One of the most popular tags people put on each other's behavior is the *complex* label. Jung first coined the term to identify how material is organized in the unconscious. Like *love, faith,* or *existentialism, complex* is so often misused we need another way to express exactly what happens in our dreamscapes. In order to clarify the term, we're going to talk about *Tornadoes* in the Wilderness.

In popular parlance, we refer to mother complexes, guilt complexes, castration complexes, and father complexes as emotion preoccupations. In a similar way, we also allude to people as having "hang-ups." These colorful terms describe obviously unresolved areas of conflict in people who are unduly sensitive or seem burdened by a recurring need. Even though *they* don't seem to be aware of persistent pressure, *we* can observe a lingering problem. Tornadoes are blowing in the Wilderness!

Highly significant experiences and unresolved problems become organizational centers in the unconscious. These emotional hubs exert a magnetic force, drawing current experiences around the old core problems. Like the vortex of a tornado, the fury and power of the storm can be overwhelming. Generally, we aren't aware that our perspectives can be shaped by the inner dust these storms kick up in our unconscious.

Discernment demands occasional weather reports on the impending Tornadoes, and our dreams provide the meteorological data on how the emotional barometric pressure is building. Like archetypes, Tornadoes exert unseen but powerful influence on our feelings, decisions, and perceptions. The storms may appear to die down but are actually only waiting for another opportune moment to return. Until the core problem is resolved, we are not free. In fact, the entire direction of one's life can be shaped by these unresolved problems.

Robert Wise's dream of being left by his parents in a cotton field might be described as an abandonment complex, or a castaway Tornado. Each time the dream returned, he was alerted that a storm was brewing. As a matter of fact, his childhood was filled with worries about not belonging anywhere. He had difficulty attaching to his adopted family.

When a dream occurs over and over, we can postulate a Tornado is loose. As twisters devastate towns, complexes can wreck emotional stability. Similarly, key issues may return again and again in different story form. For example, men often dream they are at various places without their pants on. One dream may be happening on a street corner while another occurs at a party. The structure is always the same. The dreamer becomes aware of being dressed quite properly except for one problem. No pants! The man is horrified. Even though these dreams vary, the message is the same. A fear of being exposed as inadequate or never completely prepared keeps brewing in the unconscious. Unresolved issues are crying out for resolution.

Discernment is increased by putting recurring dreams and dream themes in a larger context. When we notice a particular set of symbols (or when subjects appear with great frequency) we can bet there's a Tornado out there. Often our dream log will help us become aware of the twisters. Once we identify what's at the vortex of the storm, we're on our way to greater individuation.

Meet Robert's Twin

While Robert Wise was studying at the Jung Institute in Switzerland, he had an overwhelming dream. Arising from the whirlwinds of his past, the dream was evidence that the abandonment Tornado was still alive. The dream was so vivid, the content had to be very important.

"In the dream I am working out with weights at a health club when I look up and discover an identical twin is at the opposite end of the room. This person is exactly like me in every detail, except he's taller. I am shocked! I immediately go across the room and strike up a conversation, only to discover this man knows *everything* about me. Even though we have a long period of silent communication, I know this person is actually my twin brother. He tells me we had the same parents but we were not worthy of them. His comment is emotionally overwhelming.

"We go to my office. People come by and are astonished to meet my twin. My adoptive father drops in but discounts the brother. Other people talk to this astonishing look-alike. He finally gets in his car to leave. My spouse appears and is also staggered by our identical appearance. The dream concludes with her saying, 'Most amazing thing I have ever seen.'"

As Robert worked on this dream, he discovered there were at least two layers of meaning to deal with immediately. His first impulse was to title the dream "Finding My Twin." He wrote out the dream in the form detailed in Chapters 4 and 5, and immediately he recognized some strong and obvious meanings:

Setting

1. Health club: Two meanings are clear. A spa is a place to stay healthy—a good image for working on my life. At the same time, I am trying to maintain my physical appearance. Like pumping up my muscles, I could be inflating who I am.

2. Twin: Seems to be an alter ego, a persona. Maybe this is an image I try to present to people. Someone larger than I re-

ally am. Maybe there is some grandiosity here to compensate for the fact that I am not a very tall person in real life.

Tentative Conclusion: This dream seems to be about the image I present to people. Is it telling me that I am preoccupied with keeping up appearances all the time? Maybe I am misidentifying my physical appearance for the real me. If so, I can surmise the problem in the dream is mistaking the outer Robert for the real inner person.

Problem

1. Going to the office: I immediately go to the place where I meet people "officially." The problem seems to be unfolding where I meet the public.

2. Amazed people: People are surprised there are two of us; at least they are baffled. Some are amazed that the image and the person are different.

3. Father's indifference: Father discounts me, as was true of life experience. Reaction frustrates me. Probably represents continuing failure to meet his expectations. (When parents appear in a dream, they are usually not a symbol but themselves.)

Tentative Conclusion: I present an image of myself that isn't quite accurate. People will be in consternation by discovering there are "two of me." However, neither the image nor the real me seems to be enough.

At this point, there certainly were elements of truth in what Robert had worked out, but he didn't feel he was really going deep enough. The responses seemed too much on the surface. He had been scratching around in the dirt, but he needed to get a shovel and really go down. In order to do so, he retitled the dream "Finding the Real Me" and started over again, applying the People Paradigm more fully.

Setting

1. "I": The "I" in the dream is the Doorkeeper. I forgot to fully consider the implications of the Doorkeeper's function. Obviously the ego is being confronted by an alternative.

2. Health club: The Doorkeeper is at work building up his muscles, obviously to stay in strong control. There is a "pumping up" going on here to maintain both strength and appearances.

   But wait a minute! Is it possible the Doorkeeper is trying to become strong enough to bear the weight of the appearance of a new truer self?

3. Twin: Same-sex figures are often Shadow folks. There certainly is a shadow dimension to this twin. At the same time, the twin felt extraordinary in the dream, bigger than life. Almost numinous, spiritual. Is it possible the twin is my true self? Is the twin the real alternative to the Doorkeeper?

Tentative Conclusion: The Doorkeeper is confronted with a personal reality that would make image-building no longer a necessity. He can stop "creating illusions" and just *be* if he can accept the adequacy represented by the twin.

Problem

1. Same parents: We are biologically the same, children of the same source. However, we don't feel worthy, don't have sense of their affirmation. The problem is an old inability to

feel really accepted by the parents of origin.

Does that diagnosis ring any bells? Sound like a Tornado at work? Sure does. Abandonment.

2. People at the office: The real self has better acceptance by others than the old image. The real self gains immediate acceptance—a very positive affirming sign.

3. Father's discounting: My father's reaction would send the Doorkeeper back to the gym to pump more weights to try to become more adequate. *That reaction is a lifetime problem!*

No question about it, I am dealing with a Tornado here. Trying to be enough to be acceptable! This dream is a part of a much larger set of issues. I'm into a complex!

Tentative Conclusion: While the rest of the world is quite ready to recognize the significance of the emerging reality of my personhood, the parental components of the past aren't satisfied. I am still searching for "who I am." A part of me is still lost out in a cotton field somewhere located on the other side of the Wilderness. However, the displaced self is ready to come back and take his rightful place. The problem is the Doorkeeper is waiting to get total approval before allowing the issue to be settled.

Solution: Wife appears: Alter-Gender figure emerges with complete affirmation of the twin. The suggestion is I need to "feel" my way into acceptance of my total self. It isn't a thinking, reasoning process, but an emotional integration.

"I went back to some of my discerning questions. How is this dream attempting to bring greater unity to my life? How is this dream trying to reveal what is genuine? How is the Holy Spirit speaking to me through these symbols? Each of these inquiries helped me sharpen my perception of the message from my twin.

"Clearly, the entire dream was about discovering what is genuine. The fact that the twin was larger in stature caused me to take a second look at my gifts. I have always had a tendency to discount myself and my abilities. Sometimes this tilt came off as presumptuous and arrogant when I tried to mask my doubts. On the other hand, I generally assumed other people were more capable than I. My own gifts seemed to be so natural I tended to not give them much significance. Of course, this perspective was unrealistic and created false humility. Maturity would follow only as I embraced and became comfortable with some of the capacities I have. The dream is telling the Doorkeeper to quit working so hard on performance and let me 'just be.'

"In the dream I was seeing my true self. The size was larger because of my tendency to discount myself. My true significance is better than I thought! As these insights came forth, I felt an overwhelming sense of achievement. The affirmation was nearly euphoric. Great well-being followed. I knew I was on the right track.

"My personal unity and individuation were inhibited by my perception of a discounting parent figure. I still carried with me feelings of not being truly worthy in my parents' eyes. My doubt made it difficult for me to just 'be me.' However, in earlier dream work I had discovered this early trauma had a very fortunate side effect. The absence of a positive father figure created a craving for a transcendent Father. A great gift had resulted. I genuinely hungered to know my heavenly Father.

"The twin dream reminded me of the necessity of allowing my ultimate source of affirmation to come from God's acceptance. If the message of the twin was to be realized, I needed the spiritual help that could only be found through a personal relationship with God the Father. I could conclude the Holy Spirit was speaking to me.

"I could detect great progress was being made in breaking up an old storm. The abandonment Complex was beginning to break down. Just maybe the old, very distracting Tornado was losing its punch!"

As Robert was working on solutions, he was suddenly flooded with insight. He had reached a place in his individuation where the true self could emerge without masquerading behind images acceptable to the Doorkeeper. His full uniqueness could truly come out of hibernation.

"The dream suggested one facet of the work of the first half of my life was completed. I had achieved a new unity. I didn't have to keep searching to find out who was lost in some farm field. Abandonment fears no longer clouded my identity.

"I wept, realizing an ancient thorn was removed from my psyche. The past no longer had power over the present. I was liberated from a haunting fear. For a few minutes I basked in the glory of a life accomplishment. I had climbed a long way out of a dark pit.

"But I couldn't rest on my laurels. The dream insisted I look further. In addition to good news, the dream urged me on to deeper insight.

"I could see the need for unity in another area. The Doorkeeper was still trying to manage my life at every opportunity. We were still in a battle over who owned the turf in my spiritual and emotional world. Ego's domination was not ended. The Doorkeeper was more than happy to come up with any assortment of masks and compromising personas to meet other people's expectations. The Doorkeeper is always more comfortable with masks than the real self!

"Another question had to be reconsidered. How is the dream trying to reveal what is genuine? A new issue began to emerge. I always found it easier to keep faith with others than myself. I had to work harder at maintaining consistency with myself. The dream issue was integrity."

As Robert thought about this problem, he remembered that persons with abandonment or abuse issues are always cocked and primed to do whatever will gain the affirmation of significant others. Selling out for approval is second nature. However, the key to ensuring the true self's emergence is staying true to who we are and not to what others want us to be.

The third time Robert assessed the dream, something fresh surfaced.

"I found another problem had to be faced if authenticity was to be achieved. My father was an important figure in the dream. My childhood relationship with him had been difficult and troubled. I started looking at his involvement in the dream from a new angle.

"Slowly a different emotion bubbled up. The longer I thought about his comments in the dream, the more angry I became. There was more hostility lurking in the Wilderness than I wanted to admit. Feelings of rejection by any parent are hard to dispel.

"While I felt I had failed him, he had also failed me. I wanted a hero father who would embrace my inconsistencies as well as my triumphs. When even my best achievements didn't seem to be enough, I was left with bitter feelings. However, continuing anger would only keep the true self from emerging.

"I had to release my father from the responsibility of giving me value. Unfortunately, he just couldn't do the job. Anger would only keep me attached to him in an illegitimate mode. In fact, resentment toward anyone only keeps us under that person's control. I had to extend to my father the sympathy I needed from him. Only as I embraced him with the same acceptance I wanted could I gain the integrity of my own personhood. A spiritual reconciliation was necessary to reach the other side of insight."

You're No Different

While Robert Wise's life story may have some unusual twists, his emotional need is not particularly different from countless numbers of people who were not adopted. We develop survival fears for a myriad of causes. Childhood traumas and rejections may create an identical problem. Most of us live most of our lives with considerable misgivings about our viability.

Because of personal misgivings, we wear masks and develop alternative personalities. With time we lose any sense of who is really behind the facade. Paul and Robert once worked with a nationally acclaimed actress plagued by serious self-doubts. She changed roles so easily because there was no sense of personhood to get in the way. The actress could be anybody because inside she was nobody.

The challenge of dream work is to become a whole, integrated person. Once you've become aware of the Tornadoes, you will be able to get at the vortex of the storms. With time and work, the problem will dissolve and you will be able to respond from your true center.

Your Assignment

Take another look at the dreams you've already worked on. Maybe you have only scratched the surface and need to get out a shovel. Is more discernment needed? There might be a gold mine waiting out there in the Wilderness.

See if you can get a sense of how a particular dream might be a part of a cluster pointing toward a Tornado. Are there larger, overriding issues you need to investigate?

When you hit a nerve and discover bad feelings are lurking around the corner, stop and be honest about the relationships reflected in the dream. Is forgiveness or reconciliation or healing needed? What should happen to set you free of negative emotion? Sure, some of the territory in the Wilderness is emotionally demanding, but the rewards are great.

Out there in the backcountry you may even find your own twin. Get acquainted. You'll never be sorry. Your heavenly Father's thumbprint is there.

Chapter 8

READING THE HANDWRITING ON THE WALL
Interpretation

> *When a man begins to observe himself from the angle that he is not one but many, he begins to work on his being. . . . But if he begins to observe himself, he will then at that moment, become two—an observing side and an observed side.*
> MAURICE NICOLL, *PSYCHOLOGICAL COMMENTARIES*

Warning! Dream interpretation is not a parlor game.

The preceding pages commend the benefits and results of dream work. We hope you've found direction in identifying the messages from your dreams. However, the techniques of bringing consciousness into the unconscious are not child's play or casual recreation.

You'll notice in most of the examples we've discussed someone was seeking clarification of his or her dream. Help from a skilled and trained professional can be invaluable in keeping balance because there is always the possibility of needing assistance to confront highly threatening issues.

We sure don't want to dampen your ardor for the subject! However, we must make sure you're aware of the risks in opening up potential neurotic problems lurking in the Wilderness. Sometimes apparently normal behavior is only a mask for very severe problems or even latent psychosis. It's possible to go digging for the water line and hit a gas main!

We observed a professional woman who developed an almost inordinate interest in dream work. During this time Kathy was also going through a number of traumatic events in her life. Her dream work paralleled the emergence of unusual shifts in her personality. As Kathy became more unpredictable, she also became strangely accident prone. Broken bones and car wrecks signaled a bent toward self-destruction. Her behavior became erratic, and several attempted suicides followed.

Dream work didn't cause her problems! The woman's difficulties had been brewing since childhood. However, Kathy was a poor candidate to take a walk in the Wilderness. The Doorkeeper was not strong enough to keep the Tornadoes out of her daily life. Kathy's opening up her dreams *by herself* only made matters worse.

The fact that Kathy had a significant academic background in psychology was no guarantee of anything other than her ability to do college work. Many times people are drawn to counseling, psychology, and psychiatry because of their latent need for help.

A certain level of stability is important for journeying into the unconscious realm. People with sound mental health will become even stronger. However, persons with structural weaknesses in their personalities aren't equipped for the trip. Our feet must be planted firmly on the earth if we are going to take a walk with our head in the clouds. The problem is similar to the cause of earthquakes. Tremors result from faults in the inner structure of the globe. Unseen layers can't support the weight and pressure of the surface.

Sooner or later something has to give. Some people have unfortunate parallel defects in their psyches. Such problems demand respect.

Watch for Falling Rocks

Trail markers must be observed. Everyone needs to give some thought to these questions before ascending either to the mountain heights or descending to the depression valleys in his or her dreamscapes.

1. Do some experiences periodically cause you to go out of control? Do you blow up every now and then and *completely* lose rational command of yourself? Does it take a long time to get yourself back together? If so, dream work may not be the right road to take.

2. Have you ever been involved in self-destructive behavior? A suicide attempt? Many accidents? Do catastrophes happen too often? If so, better reconsider traveling further without help.

3. Ever have dreams erupt in violent explosions? Do you encounter frightening symbols like fire? Wild raging beasts? Cars blowing up? Special attention will be given later to nightmares. However, if your dreams feel like your head is blowing off, you have a signal to seek outside help.

4. Are you acquainted with a psychiatrist, counselor, minister? Is someone available to help you with issues arising out of dream discoveries?

Many Christian traditions train spiritual directors to help in integrating psychological and biblical insights. Such persons can help us maintain balance and perspective. You may want to find such a person to walk with you as your dream work unfolds.

Don't be frightened by the foregoing warnings, but take the admonitions seriously. Working out unresolved issues of the past is possibly the most significant work of our lives. We need all the help God and man offer. And we need to be realistic.

With these qualifications in mind, we're ready to take the next step in learning how to make dream symbols talk. We look further into reading between the lines, the art of reading the handwriting on the wall.

Tours in the Wilderness

Let's discover more about how to explore the unconscious realm and become better acquainted with the folks we meet through the People Paradigm. You may be surprised to discover a dialogue with these characters is possible! This process will be called "a tour." We've got quite a tour package waiting for you. And it sure costs less than flying to Europe! We are going to explore a technique for "dialoguing" with dream symbols. To help you get a feel of the idea, we're going to explore what happens when we daydream.

Often called "active imagination," the touring process is essentially little more than developing the art of daydreaming and self-reflection for use in dream interpretation. Most of the time we simply enjoy our flights of fancy and don't reflect on the meaning. Nevertheless, they are an important gauge of unfulfilled personal needs. What comes floating up over a cup of coffee may tell you volumes about your fears, misgivings, and current emotional imbalances.

Did you ever read the little classic story, "The Secret Life of Walter Mitty"? The humorous tale of Walter Mitty's flights of fancy into imaginary worlds of adventure and intrigue were a mirror of his own dull world of inadequacy and ineptitude. Mitty needed to pump himself up. His daydreams supplied what he didn't have within himself. We can take a clue from Walter Mitty about the meaning of our secret thoughts. Dreams encapsulate these same feelings into symbols.

Let's say I like to sit by the ocean while I fantasize about what an important man I really am. Suddenly I am the president of the United States walking into Congress as the members wildly applaud my accomplishments. Then the daydream slides into another sequel, and I am reviewing thousands of military troops standing at rigid attention. On another occasion the dreamscape shifts, and I am the president of General Motors. The heads of the major divisions of the car company are gathering in my office to await my latest insight into how the American economy can overtake the Japanese. As I explain, these brilliant men listen in awe of my baffling insights. Each episode feels warm and very comforting.

What would you guess is going on? What would you conjecture might *not* be happening in my life?

Shift the scene. A woman has just sent the kids off to school. She is sitting in the kitchen looking at the dirty dishes in the sink and wondering where her husband is. He's actually been gone on a business trip for a week. Her hair isn't combed, and she's still in her bathrobe. Her mind carries her away from the pile of dirty dishes, and she is walking along the sandy beach at Waikiki wearing a bikini minus the twenty-five pounds she meant to lose two months ago. Abruptly Tom Cruise walks up and stares at her. From the look on his face, Cruise has obviously never seen such an alluring creature. He coughs and seems to be embarrassed. The movie star is clearly intimidated by the presence of such beauty. "Please," he begs, "tell me your name. I couldn't live if I thought there was no hope I might ever see you again."

Doesn't take a lot of reflection to recognize what's happening in each of these scenes. A need for importance, power, recognition, and adventure are all possibilities. If we look at the underlying theme of each fantasy, we quickly understand something about where the person's emotions are at the present moment. Like a starving man dreaming about steak and pie, each of the scenarios describes an unfulfilled need lurking out there in the Wilderness. This dynamic will help us understand the content of our dream symbols.

Talks with Ourselves

When daydreaming we know we aren't talking to leprechauns, elves, "spirit guides," or some variety of independent demonic reality. Of course, if we really think we're talking to someone who is actually there in an invisible form, we do need psychiatric help! Quite to the contrary, when we daydream we know we are *talking to ourselves*.

While we don't give the matter a lot of attention, we are actually participating in a very sophisticated process that distinguishes us from animals. We have the capacity for self-reflection. We are both an observing and observed self at the same time. These contemplations give us distance from the control of the Doorkeeper and allow new possibilities for objectivity.

When we are angry or frightened we often go into a conversation with ourselves or someone else who isn't there. We start working the problem through by "talking it out." Our ears are able to hear what is pounding away in our hearts, and our blood pressure subsides. We get the surging passion out from between the walls of our skull into the daylight where misconception can be exposed. The sound of our voices allows us to wiggle out from under the control of our fears or hurts and get the "runaway emotion" back in the box. Again, we know we're not actually talking to invisible people or forces. We are objectifying a very subjective moment in our life.

Daydreams are possible only as long as we don't practice excessive self-condemnation. We allow ourselves a wide display of fantasy options. While we are not suggesting pondering lascivious thoughts, for a few moments we suspend the usual overpowering sense of obligation and responsibility in order to find a creative alternative to our current life dilemma. We can consider having a summer home in Colorado as long as we don't interject the problem of paying for it or think about whether such a place is a good investment. These everyday, very normal processes provide the basis for entry into the unseen side of our personalities. We are going to build on how the mechanism of self-observation operates. Hang on to this insight. We will use the approach on our tour.

Here's another exercise to help understand how the tour works. Try taking the feelings you often express in words and repacking them in image form. For example, you might make such statements as, "I am really furious with you" or "I am so upset I could kill her," or "I am so sad I think I will cry." Each of these sentences is a verbal statement of an inner emotion. Consider how you would express exactly the same sentiments with a symbol. Could you find a picture to hold up before another person that would convey exactly the same idea?

One immediate image comes to mind. Local newspapers carried a picture of a crowd of people gathered in front of a South Carolina jail as police took Susan Smith away after she was arrested for killing her two small children. The faces of the jeering crowd showed mingled horror, sadness, and livid anger. Some were ready to kill while others were overwhelmed by grief. This picture conveyed a wide gamut of emotion. If the same photo appeared as a dream, we would have to carefully decipher what the message was. The upset faces could convey anger, malice, or even shock.

Play with this exercise. Find colorful ways to express a feeling. You might depict an untrustworthy person with a split tongue as "speaking with forked tongue." If a friend betrays you, you might develop a picture of the person wearing his or her coat inside out or backward, a real "turncoat." The better you are at putting your feelings into pictures, the more accurate you will become at turning your dreamscapes back into words. You will soon discover why a picture is worth a thousand words.

Dialogue with the Downstairs

On our tour we are going to do the opposite of the previous exercise, which had you thinking of images that corresponded to words and phrases. Now we are going to put the images back into words. Our task is to do it with the utmost accuracy. Just as the picture of the jail crowd might convey many things, so most of our dream images have multiple dimensions. We are going to develop a method to decode the message more fully.

However, we must turn the dream forms into more than mere words. Words are good for starters, but they don't really hit the nerve centers. Nouns, adjectives, and verbs are only the buckets in which we are trying to carry meaning. Dreams invite us to drink from the pail. We are after insights that surpass words.

You will know when you have reached this level because the discovery will delight and confound you. Lights will go on in your head. You will find yourself flooded with understanding. We have not fully grasped what the dream is saying until this level of discernment emerges. Dream tours lead us to this place of exciting breakthrough.

There is a solid reason why talking to ourselves accomplishes so much. Remember our discovery about why dreams are possible? The Doorkeeper goes to bed as we sleep, and the door to the unconscious slips open. Without his surveillance and censorship, the material in the Wilderness is able to seep into our awareness. Since past experiences are stored as images, the dream symbols in the Wilderness appear.

Daydreams work on exactly the same principle. Although we're awake, the Doorkeeper is snoozing. The urges from the Wilderness are cloaked in pleasing and comforting apparel, so their appearance is acceptable. Our reflections are harmless, and everyone is happy.

We are going to use this same principle to take the extended tour.

Rules for Tourists

Let's consolidate what we've learned thus far. These principles make the tour possible.

1. Just as we talk to ourselves and reflect aloud, we can dialogue with the symbols of our personhood that appear in dreams.

2. These imaginary conversations work only to the degree we allow ourselves to engage in a process that seems silly at first. We have to let go and allow our unconscious the freedom to speak.

3. Remember, dreams are compensatory. They try to make up for something that is out of balance. Daydreams are the same. We must ask ourselves what deficit needs to be filled. What balance needs restoration?

4. The task is to turn our symbols into words in order that they become insights. The ultimate objective is greater understanding.

5. Strangely enough, dreams yield their meaning only to the degree their content is taken seriously. We should treat all components of a dream with respect. Each of these symbols is a dimension of ourselves. We honor our own personhood when we take the dream seriously.

All Aboard!

We're ready to start the tour, but first we must get back in touch with the dream we are exploring. Not only should we read the dream over several times but it also helps to re-experience the flow of the plot. Our notebook is before us with our dream work carefully written out. The difficult symbols have been identified and the problems for interpretation are already carefully defined. We know what we are looking for on the tour.

In our seminars we often instruct people to close their eyes and try to re-enter the dream as if it were happening all over again. Let the experience roll around in your mind for a while until you have once again penetrated the glow, the ambiance.

Our tour begins by going back inside the dreamscape. We may not be able to understand the reason for some person or animal surfacing in the dream. Possibly we're not clear about why some inanimate object has appeared. Regardless, our objective is to strike up a conversation with the mystery so we can unmask the portion we don't understand. We are going to create a dialogue with the natives to learn their secrets.

The tour is going to take us inside the world of the characters in the People Paradigm. We are going to talk with them in a give-and-take discussion as we would converse with any other person. We may even need to talk with the movie producer to clarify why a certain inanimate object was used in the story. What better source for clarification?

The dialogue will unfold in question-and-answer form. The process works best when written out in long hand. You will pose questions to the dream symbol and then write whatever response immediately comes to your mind. You will be writing the answers from the dream figure. Don't reflect on what you write; just keep the conversation going. Particularly don't think about how bizarre the whole experience may seem to be. Simply let the daydream form of discussion unfold on paper.

Let's go back to Robert Wise's "hot fudge drapes" dream in Chapter 4. He had more trouble getting the dream to start unraveling than he indicated earlier. He simply couldn't get inside the meaning of what the motion picture was suggesting. He decided he needed to go to the source. The only person who understood this symbol would be the movie producer himself. Robert needed to get in touch with him.

Robert has developed a gimmick to get the ball rolling. It's a little game he plays with himself to get tuned in. In his fantasy of the Wilderness, the entrance is a subterranean cave. He has to take an elevator located in the back of his memory to get to the cave. He simply imagines himself entering the cage by closing his eyes and envisioning the lift in as much vivid detail as possible. He pushes the down button; the elevator descends. The many floors rush past, and finally Robert comes to the bottom. The door opens slowly, and he steps out into the cave.

The place is dim, but the path is clear. Straight ahead is a makeshift reception desk with an intercom and microphone waiting for him to use. He pushes the button and asks for the person he's seeking to come out. Relaxing in the chair, he waits for his interview to begin. He lets the figure appear in his imagination, then the questions begin at once.

In the instance of the hot fudge drapes dream, he was particularly hoping for insight into the setting. So when the producer appeared, Robert said:

"I don't really understand the setting of my dream. What am I doing visiting this place where films are being made?"

Answer: "Sorry, your question is not precise enough. You need to ask differently."

Robert was really surprised at this response. He wouldn't have expected such a thought. Therefore, he knew he was on the right track since the answer had its own unique twist.[1] He said:

"Okay. What does the selection of a movie mean?"

Answer: "Good question. Robert, what does seeing a movie do for you?"

"Well, I love to go to the cinema. I guess it's sort of an escape for me. It's like . . . an experience of another reality. I get to touch another aspect of life I couldn't otherwise know. I encounter situations I wouldn't have an opportunity to live out."

Answer: "So what do you find by going to a place where movies are being selected and produced, Robert?"

Robert thought about the question. Insight suddenly followed. He realized the setting was about exploring another aspect of reality. He was at a place where he was considering entering a world he hadn't known before. He was exploring another aspect of reality he hadn't been able to live out. Now he understood the setting for the dream.

Take a look at another of Robert's dreams from a number of years ago. In the problem phase, Robert is in a bar talking with Tim, one of the men on his church staff. Another male staff member, Tal, shows up and interrupts their conversation. Tal is his usual friendly and inappropriate self with no awareness of his intrusive effect on their conversation. Robert tries to turn the intruder off, but Tal is oblivious to the interruption he is causing. The scene shifts and goes to the final solution portion of the dream. However, Robert is baffled by what Tim and Tal represent. He again turns to the movie producer for insight.

"Obviously these names, Tim and Tal, are so much alike they sound almost like twins. Please explain the casting."

Answer: "Good start, yes. But you've failed to notice how they are very much alike and also very different."

"I don't think I understand. The men seem very different to me."

Answer: "They are both quiet and somewhat reluctant; they are not forceful, assertive men."

Robert was surprised. He had not realized the degree to which these two men functioned in a very similar manner. Both worked hard to please and both avoided confrontations at all cost. Robert began to think about why Tim seemed to be so different from Tal when their resemblance was now very clear.

"Hmmm, I am surprised. Yes, they are actually sort of twins. But how are they different?"

Answer: "Why do you like Tim so much?"

"He is quiet but very competent. Even though he's not forceful, Tim is obviously quite a sincere person. I know he is genuine and can be trusted."

Answer: "What about Tal? How do you feel about him?"

"Tal is the most ingratiating person I think I've ever known. He's like a puppy wagging his tail while he's soiling your carpet. He's weak but quite divisive in the church. He's always smiling like everything is fine, and yet I know behind the gushiness is a knife. So what does this mean?"

Answer: "What does meeting in a bar suggest to you? What does a tavern imply?"

Again Robert was surprised. He would not have expected or thought up this question. He had completely overlooked a very obvious and important symbol.

"A bar? I suppose . . . a bar suggests something compromising, clandestine—something on the shady side. A place where questionable things happen."

Answer: "Then consider why you might be meeting two shadow figures in a bar. What is going on if Tal and Tim represent a dimension of your personality? What might these two figures be trying to tell you in a bar?"

Now Robert was really baffled. Obviously he was denying some aspect of his behavior he didn't want to see.

"Please help me. I just can't see it."

Answer: "Robert, you have been living at a place of compromise. You have been ingratiating rather than sincere in some of your dealings with the public. Haven't you often lamented developing a 'hail-fellow-well-met' style when you are basically a far more reserved person? You like Tim because he reflects a true side to your nature. Tal is the 'putting-on-an-act' style you keep forgetting is nothing but compromise. Tal will be whatever people want

136

him to be. That's the problem you have to face. Tim and Tal are trying to get you to face up to the charade you've fallen into. Let yourself be forcefully quiet. Let the real you emerge."

Robert was really shocked as he looked at what he had written on the page. He had completely failed to consider these two men as shadow components. He had been blind to a significant issue in his life, and he suddenly realized why he had had such conflicts with Tal, who reflected an aspect of himself he despised and yet he hadn't been able to see the resemblance. The dream was forcing him to face a personality compromise. He needed to be himself, regardless of who was or wasn't pleased.

Getting a feel for the tour? Insights are waiting for us out there in the no-man's-land in the Wilderness. Sometimes this process can help us complete a missing part of the dream. For example, Lisa came for counseling because she kept dreaming about being chased by a faceless man. She was quite sure the man meant her harm. The fact that he couldn't be identified terrified our client.

Lisa was instructed to back into the dream through the reflective process described earlier. When contact was made with the man, Lisa was to try and talk with the figure regardless of how apprehensive she might be. As soon as she let the man catch up with her, he suddenly had a face. The man was her father!

Instantly Lisa understood a very significant issue in her life. Because of past estrangement with her father, she had emotionally pushed him out of her life and refused to consider his importance to her own well-being. Lisa had ignored his existence so long he had lost a conscious identity for her. The dream was telling Lisa her estrangement had to be "faced." Do you recognize the symbolism in the father figure?

Once you get good at taking the tour, you'll be amazed at the speed with which insights come. Practice will increase your perceptiveness. You will also be amazed at how your sense of intuition develops. As you read yourself better, you will better read others!

Honoring the Dream

In our last two examples, insight suggested the need for action. In order to keep the flow of meaning coming and accomplish the purpose of the dream, it's important to act on what we discover about ourselves. Sue needed to make meaningful contact with her father. In Robert Wise's dream he should find a way to become more genuine in expressing his true self.

Often the dream will tell us what we need to do if individuation and integration are to follow. Failure to act inhibits our forward progress. Honoring the dream's message is like the farewell party at the end of a cruise.

Often the action must be symbolic. When the suggestion was made that the sister bury her brother's picture, she was given the means to realize the dream message and find release from her grief. Remember Jim's dream of Ann, the woman who passed out lemons? (She was the church member who left a sour taste with people.) To honor his dream, Jim made lemonade and consciously offered it to people he might have offended. No one but Jim knew of his little game, but it did make a difference in how he related to others. As we act out in some significant manner what we have seen, the true self is strengthened and we are changed by our actions.

Your tour isn't finished until you've planned and carried out your own farewell party.

Your Assignment

Go back to the dreams you've been working with and look for symbols you couldn't grasp. Remember, some images just won't ever open to us, so we don't have to live in perpetual frustration when something isn't making sense. On the other hand, you probably found some significant material you can still work through. Identify the dreams that feel particularly important to you.

Work out your own re-entry process. Robert Wise offered you his elevator-and-cave gimmick. You will probably be more successful by coming up with your own discoveries. Play around with what is the comfortable way for you to get back inside the dream. After you've found your path back to the Wilderness, start a dialogue.

Astonishing conversations are waiting for you.

Chapter 9

THE LANGUAGE
OF THE SPIRIT

The Bible and Dreams

Now when the sun was going down, a deep sleep
fell upon Abram; and behold, horror and great
darkness fell upon him. Then He said to Abram:
"Know certainly that your descendants will be
strangers in a land that is not theirs, and will serve
them, and they will afflict them four hundred years.
. . . Behold, there appeared a smoking oven and a
burning torch that passed between those pieces. On
the same day the LORD made a covenant with
Abram.

GENESIS 15:12–13, 17

S ome reader has to be saying, "Wait a minute! I'm
still not sure I'm comfortable with the esoteric na-
ture of this subject, the talking-to-yourself routine. Please put your
previous chapters and suggestions in context with what I'm hearing
about strange new spiritualities popping up every day. Are you
asking me to enter alternative spiritual realities?"

A friend once asked, "Every time I go in a bookstore, I find the dream books always stacked with the New Age junk. Doesn't the location mean we're dealing with bizarre stuff we ought to avoid?"

We suggested the friend become more discerning. Lloyd C. Douglas's great Christian classic *The Robe* is also carried in the same section as D. H. Lawrence's *Lady Chatterley's Lover*. Content and meaning aren't determined by some clerk's placement of books!

However, the inquirer had a point. Common perceptions can be quite wrong! We tend to see what our presuppositions program us to expect. Christians often read the Scriptures many times without noticing the prominent place given to dream experiences. Moreover, the current concern over so-called New Age beliefs may blind people to important spiritual realities genuinely offered through the Holy Spirit.

New Age?

Let's return to our friend's concern that dream books are often found with the New Age material. Exactly what does the term *New Age* mean? Unfortunately the label has come into popular usage much like "existentialism" did a few decades ago. Unpopular new ideas were dismissed by labeling them as existential. On the other hand, people who liked a new trend labeled it "existentialism," even though they had no idea what actually constituted the philosophy. Rather than referring to specific meaning, the word became shorthand for what people liked or didn't like. *Conservative* or *liberal* labels are often used in the same way. Definition becomes purely relative to the individual's taste. Consequently, nothing of content is communicated. New Age is now the new bogeyman phrase for teachings and ideas people don't like, maybe don't understand, or consider to be heresy.

What does New Age really mean? No one has written more widely about this new phenomenon than Douglas Groothuis. His books *Unmasking the New Age, Confronting the New Age,* and *Revealing the New Age Jesus* are attempts at exactitude. Groothuis says "New Age" is a catchall phrase for a new form of spirituality arising out of a Hindu-based philosophy of the world. Ranging from astrology to occult practices and seances, the ideas are quite similar to themes provided by groups practicing such beliefs as *theosophy, anthroposophy, unity,* and *religious science.*[1] Yale Professor Thomas Molnar's classic, *The Pagan Temptation,* is a sophisticated reading of the same trends in the Western world attempting to return society to ancient pagan perspectives. Molnar maintains radical "form criticism" of Scripture and the loss of the supernatural in Christian faith has opened the door for the new invasion of paganism.[2] Both men agree New Age implies a counterfeit spirituality.

Prayer is no longer talking to God but communicating with our center. New Age adherents create their own reality as well as talk with "spirit guides." Bogus revelations from the dead proclaim new and secret knowledge much as did the Gnostic of the first century. In fact, the latest twist in mass-marketing television programs invites you to call a 900 number to counsel with your friendly neighborhood psychic and receive spiritual guidance for an expensive per-minute fee.

A spin-off of the movement is renewed interest in the old fraud, astrology. Today an estimated thirty million Americans take this idea seriously. The yellow pages will put you in touch with one of the more than 175,000 part-time and 10,000 full-time astrologer fortune-tellers in our country today. Many of these people use Christian symbols even though they teach that hidden forces or deities actually predetermine our lives. Though the practice is condemned by Scripture and has been refuted by science, the business keeps growing.[3]

Obviously we are vehemently opposed to any movement that sidetracks people from a vital relationship with the God of the universe. At the same time, we believe it's important not to let the counterfeits rob us of the real thing. Misuse of spirituality by contemporary gurus and pantheists doesn't deter Christians from prayer. Neither should New Age misapplication of dream material cause us to retreat from the subject.

The approach and philosophy of this book differs from New Age thought in at least five significant ways.

1. Our focus is on hearing the One true God speak. We do not encourage esoteric exploration of the inner self. Dreams are a means, not an end.

2. We are not searching for an alternative spirituality but pursuing a pilgrimage in search of the wisdom of the Holy Spirit.

3. Our pursuit is not self-fulfillment but release from the bondage of self-absorption and neurotic egotism.

4. Our approach arises from the conviction that Scripture is the beginning and concluding authority on the meaning of ultimate reality.

5. Our method is grounded in the presupposition that self-knowledge is not the final goal. To know and enjoy our Creator is the ultimate objective of life. Dreams help us sort out truth from illusion so we can more fully understand what the presence of God is doing in our lives. We are able to identify deceptions arising from inner distortions of the truth and false perceptions.

Old Testament and New Testament heroes and the early Christians knew dreams were helpful in leading them to the center of spiritual reality. We are on the same path. Far from New Age, we are recovering the ancient footprints of the saints. Our task is to learn the language of the Spirit as they knew it.

Let's take a second and deeper look at how the Scripture views the meaning of dreams. Biblical insights will help us understand more fully our own spiritual experiences.

What Does the Bible Say?

Both the Old and New Testaments are filled with dream-related incidents. The first appearance of a dream is found in Genesis 15, where the Lord God appears to Abram in a vision and describes the great future ahead of him. In response, Abram makes a covenantal sacrifice as the sun is setting. "A deep sleep fell upon Abram; and behold, horror and great darkness fell upon him." In a subsequent dream, Abram encountered God again during another enactment of a covenant ceremony.

Following the normal procedures of the day, Abram laid out an offering on the ground to signal his acceptance of the divine agreement the God of the universe was making with him. He went to bed confident of following the rules. During the night Abram dreamed an amazing thing. Heavenly smoke and fire moved across the offering. God Himself was answering and ratifying the covenant! Something much larger than anything Abram could have imagined was at work. History would be shaped by this covenant.[4]

But consider how Abram accepted the experience. The dream was his assurance God had answered. What happened in his dreamscape was as real as any other encounter with God. What the patriarch dreamed was as valid spiritually and factually as a heavenly word written on a piece of paper.

The same was true in the next generation. Jacob met God in the night at Bethel. "And he dreamed that there was a ladder set up on the earth, and the top of it reached to heaven; and behold, the angels of God were ascending and descending on it! And behold, the LORD stood above it and said, 'I am the LORD the God of

145

Abram, your father, and the God of Isaac. . . . '"⁵ The entire course of Jacob's life was shaped by this heavenly adventure in his sleep.

Perhaps no one knew more about dreams than Jacob's remarkable son Joseph. Dreams not only predicted Joseph's preeminence but later provided the opportunity for him to rise to the very pinnacle of power next to the pharaoh. When the pharaoh was mystified by his dream of seven fat cows devoured by seven gaunt cows, Joseph was able to read the symbols as a predictor that seven years of prosperity were going to be followed by severe famine. His interpretation not only put him in a place of prominence but saved Egypt and Joseph's own family.⁶ Joseph clearly stated that he believed correct interpretations had to be linked to the mind of God.⁷

Interestingly enough, Jacob found it impossible to believe his beloved son had survived until Yahweh appeared to him in a vision.

The normative place dreams had in the life of Israel is clearly demonstrated in an allusion to the greatness of Moses. The Lord said, "Hear my words: If there is a prophet among you, I the LORD, make myself known to him in a vision, I speak with him in a dream. Not so with my servant Moses; he is entrusted with all my house. With him I speak mouth to mouth, clearly, and not in dark speech."⁸ The house of Israel was well acquainted with the important place dreams had in the religious scheme of things.

Nearly every major figure following Moses had significant dream experiences. Samuel's ministry begins with the Lord calling to the young child through a dream. And one reason for Saul's great distress when God abandoned him was that Saul no longer heard God speak in his dreams.⁹ Solomon had important dreams, as did Elijah. The Psalms are filled with dreams and dream imagery. The books of Job and Daniel give great significance to dreams.

From our brief survey of the experience of people of the Old Testament, we can conclude dreams had an important place in everyday life. Far from evil or encounters to be avoided, dreams were a normal method God used to respond to His people. While some people like Joseph were particularly gifted dream interpreters, the Jews had a general knowledge of how to interpret the messages coming through the dark speech of God. Important confirmations of God's will were communicated through this vehicle the Holy Spirit used as people slept.

And the New Testament?

The Gospels begin with dream stories. Joseph accepted Mary as his wife because the angel of the Lord came to him in a dream and told him the holy baby was to be named Jesus. Wise men were warned in dreams to avoid Herod, and Joseph was sent to Egypt in the same manner. Later, a dream informed Joseph that King Herod was dead. Through a dream Joseph was instructed to take the holy family back to Judea.[10]

Dreams and visions play a highly significant role in the book of Acts. Joel's prophecy, "young men shall see visions, . . . old men shall dream dreams" was fulfilled on Pentecost.[11] Peter's remarkable change of heart concerning the place of Gentiles in God's plan followed a powerful dream at Cornelius's house.[12] Paul received his Macedonian call through a vision that came in the night.[13]

The New Testament clearly views the dream experience as having great significance. Building on Old Testament history, the early church viewed dreams as one of the ways in which the Holy Spirit spoke to the people of God. There is no warning to avoid dreams or to consider them as an evil influence. The evidence is clear. We can proceed on with confidence.

Inspiration, prophecy, visions, theophanies, and dreams have important similarities. Each of these experiences is a different pattern cut from the same cloth. The better one understands how dreams and visions are alike, the more perceptive is our understanding of the Holy Spirit.

The foregoing has barely scratched the surface. As a matter of fact, the Bible has a sophisticated understanding of the dream process.

The Biblical Worldview

The first book in the Bible offers the most important discovery of human history. Genesis tells us the eternal Creator of the universe desires a relationship with His creation, intending to offer us insight, knowledge, wisdom, and understanding. Even with our limitations, we can be in touch with divine perspective. Dreams are a part of this holy plan.

While the current secular mind considers the physical world as final, the Bible points us toward the spiritual sphere as the place where this realm finds ultimate meaning and where eternity is found. Although we treat words as real and sensory experience as completely trustworthy, the Jews knew words are only symbols and our five senses don't begin to encompass the fullness of reality. God's world is much larger than earth or the cosmos. God is Spirit and must be encountered in spiritual terms. The Jews knew nonphysical experiences such as dreams might be even more real and significant than anything penetrating our minds through our eyes, olfactory nerves, and eardrums.

The Hebrew word for dream isn't even about sight or experience. *Chalom* means "to be made healthy or strong." The word is a comment on value, not process. The two basic Hebrew words for seeing, *marah* and *chazon*, do not fit the nice, precise distinctions for sight modern, scientifically trained people like to maintain. Visions and dreams are very much alike; Hebrew makes no clear delineation between the two. The latter happens with our eyes closed, the former with the eyelids open. The same is true for auditory experiences.

Scripture also refers to dream experiences as "visions of the night."[14] The implication is that dreams happen in our sleep, and visions occur in daylight. It is as though our night reveries punch their way through our waking moments. We can conclude both dreams and visions arise from the unconscious side of our personalities, as well as from God.

In the ancient world the spiritual and physical hemispheres weren't cut apart meat-cleaver style. God and human reality ebb and flow together in a smooth current. Physical and spiritual dimensions are equally real. Dreams are generally believed to be a bridge between these worlds.

Dreams are a natural for divine communication.

The same dynamic surfaces in biblical accounts of encounters with angels. *Malak,* or messenger, is generally used for *angel* and can indicate either a human or a spiritual conveyer of God's communication. Often the angel appeared in a visionary experience.[15] On other occasions the appearance of an angelic being was in more literal and tangible terms. From the viewpoint of Scripture it makes no difference whether one encounters God or angels rationally, nonrationally, with the optic nerves, in the unconscious, or through the human spirit.

Today we are catching up once again with a biblical understanding of reality. Since the Enlightenment and the advent of modern science, many people's capacity to experience the real world has been severely reduced. We have mistakenly made human sensory intelligence the ultimate measuring stick of truth. However, the heavenly Father is infinitely larger than anything measured by calipers, computers, test tubes, and psychological testing. Spirituality is not calculable.

Divine communication happens on a higher, more refined frequency called *spirit.* Music on FM radio and on television programs comes through our house on invisible electronic waves of energy. Why should it be difficult to believe prayer and dreams operate on a more lofty level of spiritual transmission? Radio and television require special receivers; dreams and prayer need another type. Fortunately, the heavenly Father placed spiritual receivers in our personalities. The basic issue isn't human capacity but whether we are turned on and tuned in.

Biblical people were!

Key Words and Major Concepts

New Testament writers used a variety of words to describe their wide range of spiritual experiences. Each word gives us a different dimension and increased insight into the nature of divine speech. The subtle nuances increase our perception of the dreams' place in their lives.

Blepo: See

One of the first words every Greek student learns is *blepo,* which means "to see." Generally neophytes translate the word in the same way they would read a first-grade primer: "*See* Spot. *See* the ball. *See* Spot chase the ball." But even "to see" has a much wider range of usages than we use in English. The Transfiguration is "seen" by the apostles. Yet, the same word is used by John to report what he "saw" through what he "heard" from the Spirit on the Isle of Patmos reported in Revelation 1:2 and 1:11. *Blepo* can mean a vision is "seen" as easily as one sees a beautiful sunset.

Onar: Dream

Onar comes closest to what contemporaries mean by the word *dream.* Used a number of times in the New Testament, Matthew's Gospel describes Joseph's experiences and the warning to the Magi with the word *onar. Onar* generally infers that something divine is at work in the dream. A particularly fascinating *onar* is reported in Matthew 27, where Pilate's wife warns, "Have nothing to do with that just Man, for I have suffered many things today in a dream because of Him."[16]

Horao: Vision

Horao is the verb form of the basic word generally translated "vision." However, only the context determines whether the word indicates a vision or a dream because *horao* can indicate both physical as well as spiritual encounters. *Horao* is used for both sleeping and waking visions. The word is found extensively throughout the book of Acts.

Horasis is very similar but can mean a vision seen with the eye, indicating a clearly physical experience. However, the emphasis of such a passage is on the content of the vision. In the Revelation description of horses and riders, *horasis* is used.[17]

An *aorist* passive verb derivative of *horao, optasia* is also used to indicate a vision. The emphasis is the self-revealing act of God. The Creator allows something ordinarily concealed from humanity to be seen. Luke used this word to describe an encounter with the angel Gabriel.[18]

A special word, *enupnion,* is used to specify a vision given during sleep. The word is used in the book of Acts when the prophet Joel is quoted, clarifying how the Pentecost experience was an act of prophecy fulfillment. Joel expected sleeping people would encounter God in a new and dramatic way.[19] *Enupnion* is also used in Jude 8.

Apokalupsis: Revelation

Is it possible to encounter the Holy Spirit in your sleep? The most common Greek word for revelation, *apokalupsis,* says it is. The biblical noun means "to uncover, unveil," or "to open the spiritual world to human encounter." The tarp is rolled back on God's realm, and we receive a special knowledge unavailable to any form of empirical or scientific investigation.

In the New Testament era, people believed two domains existed side by side with an uncrossable barrier between them because Creator and creature were of entirely different orders. The first Christians dismissed any form of pantheism. They knew that talking to the trees, smelling the flowers, and saying hello to Mother Nature wasn't talking to God. The only way into the divine world was by an *apokalupsis*. Inspiration, dreams, and visions were the causeways connecting the spiritual and the physical zones.

Obviously, the Bible puts a high premium on the value of dreams and encourages us to pursue "night speech." While the Scripture was written in a prescientific age before the advent of psychological language, Greek and Hebrew vocabularies assume what we call today the unconscious, subconscious, or subliminal. Experience is not divided into rational and emotional components. The seen and unseen sides of personality are part of one seamless garment. God can speak through either side of human awareness.

The Phone Line Goes Down

Where did Christians lose touch with dreams as a normal means of spiritual communication and insight? The question is not particularly easy to answer. The early church fathers certainly continued the practice of the apostles and the Jews, expecting dreams to be a means of divine communication. Paul Meier once noticed a particularly prominent set of books in the corner of Robert Wise's personal study at the church. His thirty-eight-volume set of the entire writings of the ante-Nicene, Nicene, and post-Nicene fathers covers the major literature of virtually the entire first five hundred years of the Christian era. The writings of these saints, martyrs, and first theologians define and shape Christian orthodoxy. Each volume is sprinkled with references expressing the identical view of dreams found in the New Testament.

The Shepherd of Hermas, one of the first books that didn't make it into the Christian canon, begins with a dream. Justin Martyr, the great apologist, revered dreams, as did Iraenus. Clement believed dreams came from the depth of the soul, and Tertullian wrote to affirm the significance of dreams. Nearly every major patristic figure made positive comments about dream messages. Ambrose, who converted and discipled Augustine, maintained that the Holy Spirit warned people of danger through their dreams.

The shift began with Jerome, A.D. 340–420, who is remembered for his Bible translation called the *Latin Vulgate.* After his own extraordinary dream-vision, Jerome had a change of heart. The affluent young man fled to the desert and then sought out Gregory of Nazianzen for instruction in Christian theology. Finally he settled in Bethlehem, living in the opposite end of the cave where Jesus was born. From this grotto, Jerome completed his Latin translation that was to become the canon of the Roman Catholic Church accepted into the modern period. And that's where our modern problem starts!

Jerome *mistranslated* the Hebrew word *anan* in Leviticus 19 and Deuteronomy 18, classing dreams with forbidden practices.[20] Unfortunately, his inaccuracy brought down the curtain on the rich spiritual dream heritage preceding him. Exactly why he erred is not clear, but the mistake is now rectified in the *New Jerusalem Bible* and the Confraternity-Douay version.

Anan means witchcraft or divination such as soothsaying. Anyone practicing *anan* was classed with magicians, necromancers (those claiming to communicate with the dead), and witches. The word occurs ten times in the Old Testament. In seven of these instances, Jerome translates the meaning as "witchcraft."

Strangely, in the isolated instance of the passages in Leviticus and Deuteronomy he translated the word as "observing dreams." Thus, Jerome's Vulgate condemns dream interpretation.[21] His translation tragically closed the mind of the future church.

We are not able to definitively explain Jerome's blunder, but we have good evidence to believe he acted out of concern over errors creeping into the Christian lifestyle of his day. Rather than using dreams to hear God, people were trying to use God's gift for personal profit. Much like Ananias and Sapphira's behavior in the book of Acts, people tried to manipulate God for an increase in their own fortunes. Savory, Berne, and Williams note:

> Whereas dreamwork in the early Church had focused on God's plan for the Church and how to keep the believing community nourished, nurtured, and spiritually focused, dreamwork among Christians of the fifth century had degenerated into the typical middle-class concerns of a very secure and self-centered people.[22]

Reacting to the reduction of dreams to mere fortune-telling, Jerome apparently translated his condemnation into the text. While we cannot conscience his error, we can identify with his concerns. Dreams are for spiritual, not fiscal, use!

While the Western world read Jerome's translation and retreated from dream work, the Eastern Orthodox Church took the opposite path, following the example of the great saints such as John Chrysostom and Basil the Great. Dreams continue to be vehicles for God's speech. Today we are in a position to return the Western church to biblical and apostolic practice.

Your Assignment

Go back through this chapter and note the many biblical references. Why not look them up to study the implications of each passage? You need to develop your own convictions about the propriety of this subject. Don't take our word for it; check out what the Bible says.

In addition, you might want to study key passages where dreams are a critical part of divine communication. Look at Genesis 15 and 28, Matthew 1 and 2, and look at the experiences in Acts 10.

To take a further look at how prophecy came through dreams and visions consider the following passages: Genesis 15 (Abraham); Judges 7:9–15 (Gideon); 1 Kings 3:5–15 (Solomon); Isaiah 1:1 and Isaiah chapters 2, 6, 13–23, 52–53 (Isaiah); Jeremiah chapters 1, 30, 31, 46–51 (Jeremiah); Daniel chapters 7–12; Revelation of Saint John chapters 1 (Son of Man), 2–3 (the churches), 4–5 (the victorious worship of God occurring right now), 6–20 (the judgment of the creation and the victory of the Christ).

The more you study the Scriptures the greater your conviction will become about the crucial place dreams had in the plan of God.

Chapter 10

HEARING GOD
Revelation in Dreams

I will bless the LORD who has
given me counsel;
My heart also instructs me in
the night seasons.

PSALM 16:7

In October 1959, John Freeman, an interviewer with the British Broadcasting Company, was completing a television interview with world-renowned psychiatrist Dr. Carl Jung when the announcer casually asked if Jung believed in God. Imagine the ripples Dr. Jung created in one of his last public interviews by saying something completely unexpected.

Freeman obviously expected the doctor to reflect the skepticism and agnosticism of modern science. Doubt, not faith, was the popular and politically correct posture. In the academic community, God was at best a museum object of speculation. No well-known academician had described verifiable contact, at least in scientifically certifiable terms.

The psychiatrist chuckled. "Believe?" Jung responded. "I don't believe. I know!"

Freeman was so scandalized the astounded interviewer quickly changed the subject. He completely missed the opportunity to ask what shaped Jung's change of mind and heart.

Dr. Jung, the son of a Swiss Reformed pastor, was deeply affected by his father's loss of faith. A victim of the old Liberalism of the last century, the Reverend Johann Paul Jung had died a disillusioned man. Carl Jung was subsequently troubled by the loss of vitality and experience of God in the European Protestant church. The psychiatrist knew people needed to have a personal encounter with God to become whole. While many of Jung's religious ideas are not biblically acceptable, his work with dreams led him to scientifically certified encounters with God that removed any doubt about the reality of the divine for him. Jung's dream experiences led him to teach that people could hear God and set the stage for the startled response of the BBC interviewer.

Recognizing the Master's Voice

Remember Nipper, the RCA dog listening to his master's voice on the old record player? RCA's quality of reproduction was so good even a dog could not hear the difference between the recording and his master's voice. We certainly want to hear God correctly more than a dog listening to a record player. Our task is to create profound awareness of the sound. So how does the heavenly Father speak?

Obviously, Christians affirm God has spoken in Holy Scripture and through Christian tradition. *No interpretation of a dream is valid if it contradicts the teaching of Holy Scripture.* God is always consistent with Himself. Any teaching on dreams or dream work that is at variance with biblical guidelines is to be rejected.

With these guidelines in mind, we can inquire further into how the Spirit of God moves through our dreams. Expect two modes of communication: direct and indirect.

Reshaping Our Lives

Indirect messages come through what has been previously described as subjective dreams. Probably about 95 percent of all dreams fit in this category; we are essentially dreaming about some aspect of our own life. Since God's intention is to bring us to wholeness, these dreams come to help us integrate and mature. Therefore, we have avoided suggesting subjective dreams are only psychological experiences. While the results may be described in terms of psychological adjustment, the ultimate intent is far more profound. God is indirectly reshaping our lives.

Actually, these dreams can take us to a more lofty place than can be found in any psychologist's office. The ultimate objective is the full development of the soul. Personality is never complete until the soul has emerged in fullness. Consequently, the early church did not talk in terms of self-actualization but spiritual development. Only through this route are we able to find the divine destiny God has for us. Iraenus put it this way, "He became what we are in order that we can become who he is. . . . The glory of God is humanity fully alive."

Therefore, we cannot conclude that subjective dreams do not have spiritual consequence. The ultimate questions for indirect dreams are not about self-realization or fulfillment. The bottom line is, "What is God trying to tell me about who He wants me to be?"

Previously, direct messages have been called objective dreams. Obviously a very small percent of our dreams, this 5 percent often consists of our most powerful and memorable experiences. We are aware of being directly addressed by the divine.

Touching Eternity

How do you know you have hit one of these celestial spectaculars?

The experience does not fit into the subjective mode. The dream's structure does not divide into the four-part scenario of setting, problem, because, and solution. The dream is much more direct and of a single theme.

Generally these are "big" dreams. Sometimes we may feel nearly overpowered by the experience. Usually the dream just won't go away. The images are overwhelmingly strong and vivid. We are aware of a superior wisdom beyond our own capacities.

The turning point in Saint Jerome's life came through such a dream. The wealthy fourth-century contemporary of Saint Augustine had become fascinated with the pagan classics. Even though he was a Christian, he was swayed by the sophisticated writings of Plautus and Cicero. His attraction was confronted by this dream:

> Suddenly, I was caught up in the Spirit and dragged before the Judgment Seat. The light was so bright there, and those standing around the Seat were so radiant, that I threw myself to the ground and dare not to look up.
>
> A voice asked me who and what I was.
>
> "I am a Christian," I replied.
>
> "You are lying," said the Judge. "You are a follower of Cicero, not of Christ. For where your treasure is, there also is your heart."
>
> Instantly I became dumb. He ordered me to be scourged and, along with the strokes of the lash, I was tortured more harshly by the fire of conscience. . . .
>
> I began to cry and wail, "Have mercy on me, O Lord, have mercy on me." My cry could be heard amid the sound of the lash.
>
> At last, the bystanders fell down at the knees of the Judge

and asked him to have pity on my youth, and give me a
chance to repent. The Judge might still inflict torture on me,
they insisted, should I ever again read the works of pagan....

Accordingly, I swore an oath calling on God's name: "Lord,
if ever again I possess worldly books, or if ever again I read
such, I have denied you!"

On taking this oath I was dismissed.[1]

Upon awaking, Jerome broke into tears, believing God Himself
had confronted him. The scholar returned to the Scriptures with
renewed zeal and ultimately finished the translation that was to
affect the church for centuries.

Often the details of the objective dream exactly fit everyday
life. The dream feels as if we have shifted from poetry to prose. We
may actually be related emotionally to the central person or persons in the dream. Characters don't feel like a representation of
some aspect of ourselves but rather a depiction of these actual
people. The dream message may be about a person or group of
individuals.

In addition, the symbolism often has unusual or clearly divine
connotation. The dream may have a mystical ambiance. God may
appear as light or as a great light. The setting of the dream can be a
church, a cathedral, a monastery, or a religious service. We can have
the sense we are touching the aura of eternity.

Crosses and crucifixes often appear. Since the cross is both a
symbol of suffering and of healing, an appearance during difficult
times often signals an extraordinary intervention of the Holy Spirit.
The Protestant empty cross is often a dream depiction of the inter-
section of the spiritual and earthly realms when the mystery of God
breaks in. On the other hand, the crucifix with the corpus of Christ
may describe death and rebirth. Often the dream crucifix suggests
resurrection is ahead in some area where we have known only pain,

suffering, or death. Such dreams leave us with a conviction that God has spoken to us.

A number of years before being ordained to the priesthood in the Anglican Church, Robert Wise had an overpowering dream of kneeling in prayer in an English cathedral. Towering stained-glass windows filled the narthex with glorious, multicolored light. The flags of medieval heraldry hung from the walls. Robert had a sense of being surrounded by ancient treasure waiting to be appropriated. A bishop wearing a cope and miter called Robert forth and laid his hands on Robert's head. Priests appeared and put a robe and stole on Robert's shoulders. The dream ended with an overpowering sense of call and mission. As soon as Robert awoke, he had a profound awareness of the need to seek apostolic succession in his ordination to the ministry.

Objective dreams confront and receive messages from the Holy Spirit. Let's consider the wide range of possibilities offered by these dreams.

1. Instruction.　When passages from the Bible appear, we have a strong clue about the nature of the dream. Often the verses are a clear message about some action we should take. In the first chapter Paul shared two dreams in which verses from the Bible played a very significant role. Here's another experience Paul had while teaching psychiatry and counseling in Saint Petersburg, Russia.

One evening Paul and a colleague ended up in an unusual discussion with a Russian psychologist. Andrea was an obviously intelligent, fifty-five-year-old woman who had lived through one of the most difficult periods in human history. A twenty-year-old Russian student was serving as the interpreter. As the topic shifted to spiritual topics, the psychologist emphatically said, "There's no way you two will ever persuade me there is a God!"

Paul recognized that the woman's tone was strained, her attitude defiant, and her emotional agenda had nothing to do with her professed scientific approach to life. Immediately he sensed the underlying emotion was anger. He had a hunch Andrea was projecting her repressed hostility toward her earthly father on God.

Paul asked, "How old were you when your earthly father died?"

The psychologist was shocked. "How did you know?" She puzzled for a moment. "When I was seventeen years old, he died at sea."

"He was gone a lot, wasn't he?" Paul persisted. "You didn't get to spend much time with him, right? You probably felt slighted. Left out. Unimportant. Did these many absences make you very angry?"

The Russian psychologist's eyes filled with tears. She mumbled something that seemed to be a yes.

Paul continued. "You probably weren't able to face the depth of these feelings. I'm sure you were fearful of admitting this anger to him or to yourself. When your father died, it became even more impossible to confront the anger."

Andrea nodded her head. "Yes, yes," she kept saying.

"You displaced your anger by aiming it at your heavenly Father. You couldn't allow logic to lead you to the obvious conclusion that God truly exists. Instead, you needed to fiercely deny His reality."

Andrea looked stunned. Her words came haltingly as she searched for some response. As if to momentarily divert the impact, she asked Paul's colleague, Doug, a theological question; he offered her a Russian Bible. Doug began quoting by memory a verse that very accurately answered her concern. Halfway through the passage he went blank. Even though he was quite good with memory work, he simply couldn't recall more of what he obviously knew. Even though Paul had memorized the verse in the past, he was equally unable to recall the passage. An embarrassing silence fell over the conversation.

Suddenly the young Russian interpreter impulsively picked up the Bible. Without knowing why or what he was doing, the young man opened the Bible. Without turning a single page, he read the rest of the passage Doug was trying to recall. The young inter-preter's mouth dropped. His hand started to tremble. "How did I do that?" he mumbled. "I don't know anything about this passage! I never knew it existed."

Paul offered the only possible explanation. "God."

Andrea was overwhelmed with emotion. She concluded, "Not only is there a God, He is obviously in this room tonight talking to me."

When Paul returned to his hotel room with a great awareness of joy, he went to sleep with a sense of deep satisfaction. Quite to the contrary of what he would have expected, his sleep was inter-rupted by a profoundly disturbing dream. The dream confronted him with the great discrepancy between his sinfulness and God's goodness. Past indiscretions rushed before Paul's eyes. The dream forced him to see the depth of the meaning of sin.

Paul cried out, "I am a sinful man! I certainly have no right to be used to help so many people here this week. I am not worthy of the miraculous things I have seen."

Even though his eyes were tightly shut and the room was pitch black, Paul had a wondrous sense of light shining through his eyelids. He felt God was speaking to him using the words of the apostle Paul, "My strength is made perfect in weakness."[2] As the phrase rolled over and over in his mind, Paul drifted back into peaceful sleep then awoke the next morning still thinking about that wonderful verse of Scripture.

That morning after breakfast, one of the educators in his group led morning devotions. The teacher began, "Last night as I was sleeping, I felt the Lord was speaking in my dreams. I want to share the passage that was impressed on me during the night." He began reading, "My strength is made perfect in weakness." Only then did Paul tell the educator that God had shown him the same verse that preceding night.

The timing of the identical dream messages was obviously unusual. Often synchronicity is also a hallmark of the direct dream. Paul knew the entire experience reflected the direct work of God.

2. Clarification. One of the most valuable aspects of either direct or indirect dreams is their capacity to bring clarity during times of confusion and upheaval. Often we will have missed relationships and connections between people. We may feel confounded until a dream gives us some unusual clues about what's "going on." When the insight is from God, we really are able to get back on track.

A lady we worked with came seeking help during a time of considerable upheaval in her church. Rose was concerned her church might collapse because of controversy created by rumors and innuendoes raging through the congregation. Rose was struggling to separate truth from illusion. Who and what were behind the confusion? At the height of the problem, she had this remarkable dream.

Rose's dream started with her standing in the parking lot of her church. A small circus tent was set up in the middle of the lot. People were entering through the raised flap. However, Rose could see only three or four actual spectators inside.

Performers entered in various costumes. Rose quickly recognized them as all being members of one family in her church. A ringmaster appeared in the center ring with a whip in hand. As the performers came forward, the ringmaster moved them from ring to ring, cracking his whip and commanding the people.

The performing family went through various routines. One was a juggler and another a clown. One daughter-in-law was trying to walk a tightrope. They were putting on quite a show. As the acts finished, the ringmaster turned toward Rose and smiled. She immediately recognized him as the associate pastor of the church! After he walked away, the tent collapsed in a cloud of sawdust on the performers and few spectators. In the background the church stood as strong as ever.

Rose's dream immediately ended her consternation. The small tent and the few spectators clarified that the big confusion came from a small group. Only one family and a few spectators were involved. Rose suddenly was aware that the associate pastor was a key part of the sabotage going on in the church. His exit would bring the turmoil to a conclusion. Amazingly enough, a couple of weeks later, the ringmaster resigned and the "tent collapsed." With his departure the troublemakers left, and the church was even stronger than before.

Rose had little trouble working through her dream because the characters and meaning were so obvious. She had great relief in knowing the problem was really only a smoke screen. Rose felt she could pray creatively and rest easy during the time of transition.

3. Direction. One of the common characteristics of the dreams in the Bible was the way God directed people like Abraham and Joseph to the paths they should take. Direction may take many forms ranging from business decisions to handling personal needs. Reassurance and hope may be offered.

A number of years ago Robert Wise went through a period of considerable personal loss and trial. His world was turned upside down as he worked through overwhelming turmoil. During this time he had a remarkable dream.

"In the dream I was asleep in my own bedroom on the second floor. I had built the house and still live in the same place. Everything about the bed, the room, and the house was exactly as it was then and is today. Three men awoke me and pointed out of the window. One man said, 'Everything that can be shaken will be shaken.' I was aware the statement was like a biblical passage and the three men were holy. I remembered the three men who visited Abraham by the oaks of Mamre. Even though I wasn't sure of the meaning of the moment, I knew I was being given a very special message.

"Suddenly the house began to quiver. As I looked out the window, the land began to move up and down in waving motions, like carpet being shaken. Trees started flying out of the ground, and I knew I was in the middle of a terrible earthquake. The entire house began to sway violently. My large waterbed lifted off the floor, and I was so terrified I began to scream at the top of my lungs. Even though I was still asleep, I could feel my heart pounding. The three men disappeared, and I remember thinking, 'I will not survive this ordeal.' From somewhere a voice answered, 'Oh, but you will. You are coming to the greatest time of your life.' The house turned on its axis and faced a new direction.

"The tremor subsided and the house settled on a new foundation. I looked out the windows at the fields beyond the edge of my property and was amazed that the terrain had completely been rearranged. Trees, lakes, and roads were totally different. Everything was peaceful and well ordered."

During the difficult days following his dream, Robert had a profound inner knowing that God was still directing his life and leading him to a place he had never been. The dreamscape offered tremendous assurance that when the time of shaking was over, the better days would emerge. And so it came to be.

4. Discernment. Sooner or later the question is raised about the possibility of confronting evil in our dreams. Usually the concern is about being seduced or deceived by evil appearing as light. Quite to the contrary, an encounter with evil is either frightening or comes as a warning. Fear, not seduction, is the order of the night.

At this point we are not considering nightmares. This special form of dream will be explored later by itself. Sexual dreams don't fit this category either. The meaning of sexual liaisons in dreams is generally far from what we immediately assume; these mirages will also be looked at later. Rather, we are considering the phenomenon of evil as an independent entity. The dream can give us insight into this pressure and these attacks on our lives.

One of the most graphic examples of breakthrough comes from the life of John Newton, the composer of the beloved hymn "Amazing Grace." For many years Newton was a slave trader bringing human cargo from Africa. Night after night he went to sleep hearing the moaning and groaning of dying men and women suffering in the hold of his ship. Finally the collective evil of years of abusing fellow human beings erupted in a violent dream confronting Newton with the meaning of the evil he was helping to perpetuate. His dream was the turning point in Newton's life.

> The most remarkable check and alarm I received was by a dream. Those who acknowledge scripture will allow that there have been monitory and supernatural dreams, evident future events: and those who are acquainted with history and experiences of the people of God are well assured that such intimations have not been totally withheld in any period down to the present time.... I cannot doubt, from what I have seen since, that it had a direct and easy application to my own circumstances, to the dangers in which I was about to plunge myself, and to the unmerited deliverance and mercy which God would be pleased to afford me in time of my distress.[3]

Shortly after writing this description of his dream, Newton became a priest in the Anglican Church. In time, his reputation for godly counsel and his hymns caused him to become one of the most revered clergy of the nineteenth century. He believed the effect of the dream was to deliver him from destruction.

Here's a different form of the same effect. Meg came with a dream that repeated itself in different shapes for several weeks but always with the same final message. Usually she was in a house looking out the windows while violent people kept trying to break in. Sometimes the intruders were burglars and other times enemy soldiers. However, at the end of each dream, she could see evil, ghostlike shapes buzzing around the house, seeking a place of entry. Meg was frightened.

After a few minutes of explanation and exploration of the dream, Meg began to get the point. Since a house is almost always a representation of ourselves, she could quickly see her life was under attack. Reluctantly, Meg admitted to flirting with the use of crack cocaine. In addition, her sexual behavior was on the verge of complete irresponsibility. Meg looked at the bottom line in her dreams and nearly panicked. What she considered as a walk on the wild side was clearly an invitation for evil to enter and destroy her life. Dream work changed the course and direction of her life.

On the other hand, consider this bizarre dream. What would you do with such an encounter? A pastor came for help with a savage dream of his assignment to the body-removal detail in a Nazi concentration camp. Jack was stacking the corpses on top of each other until the pile was so high he and his helper had to sling the bodies up to the top. While the pastor could not understand any of the meaning of the dream, he knew in some way hundreds of good and innocent people were being slaughtered.

None of us were able to give him much help with this strange dream, which didn't seem to have a middle or an end. The only obvious clue was everything in the experience was evil.

A month after trying to understand the dream, Jack's church erupted in a fight. His credibility and integrity were attacked, and he had little defense. His enemies had organized their assault on him with the skill of an SS raid on the Warsaw ghetto. The large church Jack pastored plunged into turmoil. Good people Jack had brought to faith fell away in confusion and disillusionment. At that point, Jack realized the dream was a warning of the conflict already under way before the public dimensions of the church split were known.

In each of these instances, the discernment of evil and the presence of the demonic served as clear warnings to watch out. Bad things were about to happen to good people. Usually once the warning is recognized, the person will quickly understand what needs to be done to prevent further intrusion of evil.

5. Prediction. Obviously the most alluring of all dream forms, predictive dreams are actually quite rare. People often mistake a subjective dream as having a futurist dimension. For example, if we dream of having a car wreck or of our house burning, the warning probably has far more to do with how overextended we are than the possibility of fire or of crashing the car tomorrow. In a great many instances people are not able to identify a predictive dream until the event has passed. *Therefore, we might conclude the purpose of the predictive dream is not to cause us to anticipate the future as much as to recognize the work of God when it comes to pass.*

For example, Archbishop Randolph Adler, primate of the Charismatic Episcopal Church, had a remarkable dream of a friend buying a new gray Cadillac. He looked at the odometer and noted the mileage read 1,648. As the archbishop admired the car, the friend said, "Here are the keys. It's yours." Much to Adler's surprise the same friend called the next day and wanted to drop by, saying he had something to show the archbishop. When the man drove up in a gray Cadillac, the consequence was almost overwhelming. Nevertheless, the archbishop said nothing but stopped to admire the beautiful car. At the urging of the friend, he slipped behind the wheel, only to note the odometer read 1,648. The friend placed the keys in the archbishop's hands and said, "It's yours. My gift for all the good things you've done in my life."

While predictive dreams may be intended to help us recognize the work of God rather than accurately portraying the future, history does record some remarkable exceptions to this understanding. Shortly before his assassination, Abraham Lincoln dreamed of a coffin lying in state in the White House. When he asked a guard about who had died, he was informed, "the president." At least two passengers on the *Titanic* dreamed of the disaster before the voyage began. The one who canceled his ticket survived! More often, dreams of death and dying are actually about metamorphosis within the individual.[4] (More will be said about these symbols of transformation in a later chapter.)

Dreams of personal death are usually surrounded with a profound knowing of the meaning of the dream. In one of Jung's last dreams, he saw a large, round stone with the inscription: "As a sign unto you of Wholeness and Oneness."[5] In these incidences, the dream seems to be helping us to plan and prepare.

Biblical guidelines suggest predictive dreams may appear when some dimension of God's plan is at stake. The content of such dreams puts people into an observant posture, which is important for anticipating what to do as difficult unforeseen circumstances emerge. On the other hand, predictive dreams may give us a road map and encouragement as a new and important work of God unfolds.

Paul Meier had the opportunity of working with one of America's foremost evangelists. Paul provided medical care for the elderly evangelist, whose ministry years earlier had included national meetings as well as work at higher-education institutions. During one of the crusades, the evangelist stayed in a local hotel. His dream of the hotel burning was so vivid and frightening, he got out of bed, packed his suitcase, and checked out of the hotel. In the middle of the night he moved into another hotel down the street. The next morning, the evangelist awoke to discover the first hotel had burned to the ground!

In the autumn of 1974 Robert's friend Retha had a remarkable dream. At the time her church was operating a school, and she was on the staff. Everything seemed to be going wonderfully. Retha described the dream in these terms: "My normal dream pattern was interrupted by a separate dream, which seemed set apart as if enclosed by special brackets or parentheses. Never had I experienced such a dream in which each part was so complete and every detail defined with such precision. A great scroll seemed to unroll with a series of events all going on at the same time. I seemed to be seeing a multimedia production of future events.

"The first event on the scroll was a very stressful congregational meeting. The church was divided over the continued operation of our parochial school. The next event was a gathering of parents declaring undivided support for the school and insisting the staff continue offering Christian education. In the next event I saw the school continuing with three divisions: elementary, junior and senior high, and special education. The following event on the scroll depicted an exciting, normal school functioning with great success. The final event showed me three students who were then sophomores. The girls were outstanding, but the boy was a difficult hippie type. As I looked at each person, the scroll snapped shut, and I woke up.

"The dream was so powerful I shared it with my husband and the headmaster. After a brief discussion the normal routines of the school continued. The headmaster didn't seem particularly impressed. Three weeks later he showed up at my doorstep in a state of shock. The headmaster had just discovered the church was about to split over the continuation of the school!

"In the following weeks every aspect of the dream unfolded just as I had foreseen. In the years that followed, the rest of the dream was also fulfilled. The three students turned out to be representations of why the school existed. One girl became the outstanding academic achiever in the state, the other girl helped the school develop a healthy student body life, and the rebellious boy's life was changed by the school. Today he is a pastor in California. I believe the dream was a literal message, warning us of the conflict and calling us to see the wonderful future planned for our school."

Retha's dream was a source of major encouragement during the important time of transition as the school left the church and went out on its own. Today the school is an outstanding institution in a metropolitan area.

Archbishop Adler had another remarkable dream during the 1979 storm season on the Florida coast. Weather forecasters predicted a major hurricane was going to slam into the area where the archbishop was living. The situation was tense, and concern was high.

That night his dreams revealed a remarkable sight. Spread out before him was a large map of the Florida coast. Adler watched the tempest move along the map, missing Orlando, skimming along the coast, and then suddenly turning and go out to sea.

His dream gave Adler a motion picture of what was ahead. He awoke the next morning with a profound sense of what was going to happen. The next few hours proved the meteorologist wrong and Adler's dream to be right.

Why do such dreams come to some people and not to others? There is no answer. Perhaps, the same dream opportunities were open to many people, but only those individuals were tuned in. On the other hand, some persons seem to have a gift, just as others paint or write. Others blame God for dreams He had nothing to do with. We are not dealing with an algebra formula but with the mystery of God's grace. Predictive dreams appear because of their own inscrutable logic. But they can certainly make a difference.

Paul recently discovered just how great the difference can be. His eighty-six-year-old mother had an important dream when she was twenty-seven. At the time, Elizabeth Meier was being pursued by a young man who left her feeling rather ambivalent. One night a romantic full moon filled her dreamscape. The moon looked like a giant, wonderful fishbowl with goldfish suspended in the sky. The image left Elizabeth with an overpowering sense of well-being that a happy, loving marriage was just ahead.

The next day Elizabeth shared the dream with her friends at work. As they were laughing about her impending romance, someone knocked on the door. To her surprise, Elizabeth discovered a visitor had returned out of her distant past. The young man had grown up with her in a German community in Russia, but they had not seen each other for over a decade. Elizabeth couldn't believe her ears when the brash youth said his long journey was for one reason, to ask her for a date. Alex Meier didn't waste any time. In one week they were engaged.

Sixty years later, Mrs. Meier still believes the dream was prophetic and wonderfully accurate.

Your Assignment

Do not be surprised if you don't find any direct communication among your dream work so far. At the same time, look carefully at the structure of any dreams that won't fit the subjective mode. Possibly they will fit into one of the five categories we have defined for objective direct dreams.

Since the speech of God comes both directly and indirectly in your dreams, go back over the dream work you have completed to date and take a second look at what your solutions indicated. Re-think your discoveries in light of the foregoing.

Have you stopped too soon in working on your subjective dreams? Is it possible there is still another level of exploration to be done? Look over the scope of your work and see if you can get any hints about where the Holy Spirit is trying to bring you to new wholeness. The final step in dream work is to pray over your discoveries. Where do you need to make intercession?

Chapter 11

TRANSFORMATION
Tools for Change

I do not have much success in my inner work. No sooner do I step out of my door, or arrive at the office . . . than all my inner resolves are forgotten. I lose my way. I react mechanically. I become a slave. I am pushed around by my impressions. Events take charge and my inner aim disappears. Some external aim takes its place. I become a different person.

ROBERT S. DE ROPP, *THE MASTER GAME*

While holding a seminar on family life in St. Louis, Paul Meier had an usual dream. In his dreamscape, Paul was lecturing to Germans born after 1945. Paul told his audience they should not only have compassion on the Jewish race but do everything possible to compensate for what happened to them during the period of the Holocaust. "At the same time," Paul instructed his students, "we do not carry personal guilt of what Hitler did. We were not there, and the actions of the Nazis are not our fault."

The next day Paul gave careful thought to this unexpected message. Paul had not only traveled annually to Israel but had also conducted counseling classes in Tel Aviv to help troubled Jews. There was no reason for him to feel any guilt. He began to remember his reaction to the movie *Schindler's List*. The film was so overwhelming Paul had wept heavily and had had trouble breathing during the scenes of great pain and suffering. Paul certainly had significant compassion for Jews.

Oh yes, the name *Meier* is obviously as German as you get.

Paul couldn't set the movie aside after leaving the theater. The scenes remained etched in his mind and burned in his soul. Slowly, Paul began to see his dream seminar was actually for *his* own benefit.

Paul's remorse for the Germans' treatment of the Jews was *too* personal. False and inappropriate guilt was creeping into his thinking. His concern for persecuted Jews had become internalized and self-accusatory. The dream reminded Paul his ethnic heritage did not condemn him for what others had done in a past time and place.

The dream seminar instructed Paul to lighten up, not to judge himself for the atrocious actions of others. The experience was a healing dream of transformation.

Becoming Whole

No one escapes the jagged edge of the knife of experience. We are all wounded people. Sometimes we are guilty; sometimes we just *think* we are guilty. Regardless, the need for inner healing is universal.

Never underestimate your capacity to hide the truth from yourself. We have a fierce capacity to deny what we don't want to face. Paul experienced this tenacious tendency in a patient with a problem of depression.

Assuming the source of the problem was either repressed anger or guilt, Paul probed the young man's experience in recent months and past years, but George was confident no reason for resentment or repression existed. He could see no justification for regret from any experience he could remember. Paul then suggested George work on remembering his dreams to see what surfaced.

George returned with a strange dream. He was hitchhiking and was picked up by a couple in a car with a frame, but no body. The sides of the car almost didn't exist. As the car rolled away, George sat next to the wife until a bump pushed the husband from behind the driver's seat, and George took control of the automobile. The man went running down the street, trying to catch up. After a while, George stopped and let the man back in the car. Then the couple drove off, leaving George on the road feeling lonely. George recognized the other people in the car as a husband and wife he had lived with for a short time several months earlier.

Paul had immediate insight into the dream and asked George about his relationship with the wife during the time he had lived with the family. George rather casually admitted that he did slip into a sexual affair with the wife during his stay but saw no reason for the experience to be the source of depression. Was George kidding himself, or what?

Since an automobile is a strong symbol of our selfhood, the dream cried out for George to face up to his part in pushing the husband out of his proper role with his wife, even though the marriage itself was weak, like a car with no body. Even though George didn't want to assume responsibility, the dream insisted he face his guilt. The price for not being up-front was a big dose of depression.

Why do dreams present us with a problem and a solution segment? Why are conflict and unresolved confrontations such persistent themes? Because the pain of the past cries out for release and repair!

At some point during a critical time in our development a hand grenade was tossed into our souls. The explosion sent us into emotional shell shock from which we eventually recovered. Yet long after the smoke cleared, the sound waves still reverberated through our minds. Time did not dissolve the shrapnel buried in our psyches. Like old puncture wounds far beneath the sealed surface, the contamination works away like a psychological time bomb. Scars cover the old injury but cannot keep unseen infection from pumping into our spiritual and psychological lives. Unless we have soul surgery, we may spend our entire lives compensating for the damage.

Here's another vantage point for considering the meaning of our dreams. Dreams can be surgical instruments for correcting emotional damage, putting us in touch with problem areas long since submerged from sight. Consequently, it is helpful to look at the final solution section of the dream as a source of damage control and correction. Here are several areas that often need attention and some suggestions for how we can operate on segments of the past.

Nightmares and Other Animals

These galloping horses of terror come thundering through at two in the morning, creating screams of horror and agony. The problems cry out for resolution. In order to understand night terrors, we need to make several distinctions.

Let's start with the variety called *incubus* dreams. Children are particularly victims of these attacks and wake up choking, screaming, or shaking. No one seems to entirely understand this phenomenon, which seems to be essentially physical in origin and is relatively rare. Usually we do better to reassure a child and leave the content of the dreams alone. They pass.

Adults hit one of these heartstoppers occasionally but without lingering consequence. Generally there isn't enough dream material even to dissect an incubus explosion.

Recurrent nightmares are another matter. These dreams have no final resolution or solution. They drive us to the edge of disaster just before we wake up. Generally an overpowering trauma lingers behind the scenes. We can't get at the source of the injury because the Doorkeeper is too terrified of the original experience to allow work to be done on the problem. Until we are able to locate the old terror, we can't get off "dead center."

To distinguish between the infrequent incubus dreams and the nightmares that signal the need for emotional surgery, we will call the latter Dead Centers. Unless transformation occurs, these experiences not only do not resolve themselves but return often. Our first course of action is to determine where they come from.

Remember Robert Wise's terrifying dream of being left in a field as a small child? Originally his abandonment dream stampeded over and over again like a herd of runaway horses.

We always have to consider whether such traumas indicate a split in the personality. A good rule of thumb is that the more severe the recurring dream, the more severe is the split. By the same token, these experiences may not represent a division at all. The problem may lie in a highly threatening person or a situation in our immediate environment. We must discover the source of fear. Either way, out of Robert's own experience comes good news for all of us. Any tearing in the personality can be healed, and transformation is possible.

Similar to the way a declining hurricane is downgraded to a tropical storm, in time the contents of Robert's childhood dream became downgraded enough to be more familiar and bearable. With that change in feeling, Robert could begin to poke at the content of the dream and see what might come up. Eventually, he conjectured some event was back there. The issue was whether he had actually been left in a field or the field was a symbol of another experience. This change in tone was a step toward getting the problem out in the open. Working on the dream at least had taken a considerable amount of the fear out of the experience.

"As an adult I had many dreams of being chased, pursued, or attacked by a wide range of frightening figures," Robert said. "This form of nightmare is relatively familiar. After working with dreams for a period of time, I began to see many of the chases were directly or indirectly related to the abandonment dream.

"About ten years ago I was at a conference in Glendale, California, with a group of clergy. I dreamed I was helping a boy escape. One of the clergy, one who held a rigid, legalistic view, started chasing the boy. A girl appeared and warned that Reverend Jones was after both of us. I realized he was getting closer and closer. Just as Jones was about to grab me, I confronted the man and warned him he'd better back off. A fight ensued, and to my surprise, I subdued Jones rather easily. Holding him on the ground, I put a barbed-wire harness on his face and warned him the barbs would hurt if he moved. I demanded that Reverend Jones not try to catch me again. I awoke reassured I was stronger than I thought.

"My chase dreams had a common theme, a desire to escape being trapped in prisonlike circumstances. I knew this had a connection with being adopted. Imposed authority represented internal conflict. Many actual childhood family incidents felt like being chased by the punitive clergyman. Even though the chase dream was frightening, working through it assured me I could confront and overcome my fears and apprehensions."

Here's a different angle on chase nightmares. In Calvin Hill's book *The Meaning of Dreams,* he writes:

These are all punishment dreams. For what reason is the dreamer being punished? Because he has violated one of the commandments of his conscience. He has rebelled against authority, or he has gratified a forbidden wish, or he has committed a misdeed. The nightmare is the price he pays for doing something wrong. Such dreams provide us with information about the dreamer's conceptions of the penalties that will be inflicted upon him should he disregard his conscience.[1]

If you find yourself in such dream patterns, you don't have to assume you've been caught in some overwhelmingly gross behavior. The issue is how you've violated your *own* internal code. You may have given in to a forbidden emotion such as anger or fear. Somewhere along the way those particular feelings were denied to you. On the other hand, you may be kidding yourself that you can get away with a serious moral violation. Your inner world is protesting and won't let up the accusations until you face and change your behavior.

Here's an opposite and unexpected twist. Chase nightmares may have very surprising *good* implications. Robert Wise remembers such a recurring dream.

"Several years ago I kept dreaming of a leopard pursuing me," he recalled. "I would wake up in terror that I was about to be lunch for this ferocious creature. After a long talk with my spiritual director, I attempted to condition myself to confront the animal should the dream return. Sure enough, in a few weeks the chase was on again. To my amazement I realized I had an alternative as the animal bore down on me. I stopped and confronted the attacker.

"'What do you want?' I demanded.

"To my astonishment the leopard answered, 'I thought you'd never quit running. I want to give you leopard power!' (Of course, the imagery and language is symbolic.) The Dead Center became a power source.

"Only later did I realize the dream was a gift from my shadow. I was running from new strength and capacity being offered from a part of my life I denied and rejected. Rather than self-punishment, the chase was a gift. Almost always dreams point to the possibility in the problem."

In all animal dreams we must look carefully at what the creature represents. When the animal creates fright, we need to pinpoint the origin of the fear. Were we ever bitten or traumatized by such an animal? Did we have a pet like the symbol? Could something have happened to the pet? In sorting out the meaning, we look critically at the nature of what is represented. For example, leopards and mountain lions are thought of as attackers or assaulting from hiding. Is something lurking out there? In contrast, a rhinoceros charges ahead like a bulldozer. Are we about to be run over by someone? Maybe we need to buck up and become "hard-chargers" ourselves.

Animals may represent traits we need to develop or acquire. The appearance of these symbols may offer new energy to empower us. An eagle suggests great power to soar to new lofty heights while a dove is a better picture of gentleness and peace. A fox may offer slyness, and a dog can be a faithful companion. Creatures from the zoo or menagerie may appear in our dreams bearing gifts.

Taming the Beasts

What can we do to get these wild horses under control? How do we transform the Dead Centers?

One approach has already been suggested. We work at developing a conscious intention to take back into the recurring dream. In broad daylight we come to a decision about what needs to be confronted and resolutely intend to do so when the dream returns. Like teaching a child to defend himself or herself against the school bully, we equip the Doorkeeper with new alternatives for facing the trauma hidden in the Wilderness. The Doorkeeper receives new vitality through our careful and supportive analysis of his dilemma.

In order to strengthen the Doorkeeper's hand, we need to pinpoint the emotion creating the Dead Center. What's at the bottom? Anger? Fear? Guilt? Once we are clear about the energy motivating the chase we have a clue about whether the need is confrontation or understanding, defiance or compliance. In the case of Robert Wise's leopard dream, he concluded the problem was fear of being overpowered by an emotion he couldn't control. The insight helped him decide to look the "cat" in the eye.

This technique works because a high percentage of the time the pursuer is a friend only disguised as an enemy. The problem lies in the Doorkeeper's perception. Once reconciliation occurs, the whole scenario changes. By recognizing the game going on with the assumed adversary, we can change the rules. Persistent pursuit of the pain or problem will pay off!

On the other hand, Dead Centers are so difficult because they offer no resolutions. We awake without relief. The issue within our psyches is incompletion. We need to write the end to the cliff-hanger. Here is another dream technique to help. We begin with dream re-entry and return to the dreamscape. Similar to our instructions in Chapter 8, we suggest you take another tour into the Wilderness. We suggest you visualize the dream experience as completely as possible and pay great attention to every detail. We suggest praying your way through the trip. As you reflect, keep asking the Holy Spirit to be your guide and friend along the trail.

Once you are really into the dream, let the story line sweep you along. However, don't stop when you come to the place where the original dream ended. Let your imagination keep on pushing ahead. You're not trying to make up an ending as much as you're pushing the dream energies onward to complete the action naturally.

At the point you begin to feel terror or fear, call on the Holy

Spirit to help you keep on course. With your eyes closed, go on to whatever the logic of the dream reveals. When Dead Centers find resolution, they generally offer new capacities or become healing dreams.

We can best illustrate the technique by another of Robert's dreams involving pursuit. "The dreamscape starts in a small town where I am buying a house for investment purposes. A little child pursues me, and I try to avoid being caught. I'm in the town hall, where a parade is about to start. No matter what I do, the child keeps pursuing me. I run and hide in a filling station, but the child won't let up. I keep running until I get to another street.

"This dream occurred the night I returned to the Pecos Monastery for a retreat. Pecos is a small town, and I always work on my investment in myself when I am there. The setting was clear. A little reflection on the parade symbol caused me to realize how much I wanted to impress my spiritual director with the progress I was making in dealing with my inner life and developing Christian maturity. I was really ready to get down to work . . . but the child was getting in the way!

"As I thought about the child, I became aware of how much I was neglecting an important part of my life. My little child within did get negated quite often, just as had been true of the day when he was abandoned in the cotton field. The child needed to be recognized. My tendency was to ignore these issues by pacifying and placating this area. I needed to fully embrace this piece of my past.

"Using the approach of carrying the dream forward, I re-entered and slowly walked through the dreamscape. The chase started again, but at the end of the sequence I didn't cross the street. I sat down and invited the child to come close for a conversation. My notes reflect that my talk with the child went something like this:

"'Look, kid, why are you following me?'

"'Are you afraid of facing me?'

"'I don't know. I don't know who you are.'

"'I'm the one who was left behind. Remember?'

"(I feel uncomfortable, uneasy.) 'I don't understand.'

"'Yes, you do understand. You just deny the fact you're always running away from facing me, not confronting what I'm about.'

"'What do you want me to do?'

"'Use this time to get to know me. How about just playing with me? You really don't have to be afraid. I simply need to have a little attention and nurturing. I yearn to be wanted. I can be your friend.'

"Suddenly I knew how to spend these days of retreat. I asked the Holy Spirit to help us—the child and me—work things out. I needed a new relationship with myself."

When we find a new ending for a Dead Center, it is very important to write it down. We need to reflect on the implications. As always, we honor the dream and its meaning. Offering a prayer of gratitude is also significant. Healing inevitably follows.

Transcending the Tension

Now that we have learned how to transform one of the most frightening dream types, we need to recognize a fundamental truth about the nature of maturation. *Some issues can't be changed; they have to be transcended.* This chapter began with Robert De Ropp's observation that our best intents are frustrated by the complexity of modern life. He further writes, "Multiplicity of selves is the common condition. Existence of a single 'I' corresponding to a single aim and a single will is the exception rather than the rule."[2] To become a whole person in our kind of world takes a near miracle. But then again, all transformation is on the marvelous side!

One of Jung's most insightful discoveries was that most of the truly significant problems of life are basically unsolvable. They can't be fixed but must be outgrown. Rather than our neuroses being healed, in time they will heal us. Issues that afflict us the most have the greatest potential to drive us to the wholeness we most fervently seek. While our tendency is to suppress these problems, once released they offer the answers needed for maturity.

Possibly there is no better example of this principle than Alcoholics Anonymous. Members admit they are powerless over their addiction but set out to get their lives in order. While they can't make alcoholism go away, in time a multitude of character defects are addressed and healed. The incurable illness cures the person.

In a similar vein, tragedy may visit us with painful losses that can never be restored. Yet, as we struggle with the unfillable hole in our lives, we are brought to a new relationship with God that didn't exist before. While nothing justifies the deprivation, the gain is of inestimable worth. Physical or psychological pain produces spiritual healing.

The transformation function of dreams helps us find the step-ladder to come to this utmost level. By granting us a more lofty plateau for perspective, we don't change as much as leave the past behind. When irreconcilable emotions are in conflict and collision, we have no choice but to take this higher path.

Often the transcendent function emerges as a dream image. Working with this unique symbol, we discover how the inner logjam can be broken.

Interestingly enough, another attack dream took Robert Wise to one of these amazing transformation points. "The dream opened in the middle of a terrorist assault. I was barely able to escape to a train station and catch a departing train. When I got off in another town, I was met by a clergyman I had known in the past. He immediately took me to the house of another friend, a college professor. They led me outside to meet a man in the backyard. The new man was unusually tall but as we talked he kept increasing in height until he towered over all the houses and could look across the whole town. The dream ended with the giant telling me his name was Mr. Long View.

"After much reflection I saw the telescoping man was a symbol of transformation. Without taking apart the rich complexity of the dream, the image was clearly a signal for what must happen if I was going to get beyond a certain level of personal struggle. I needed to put a number of issues 'into perspective' by taking 'the long view.' I had to get *above* the old conflicts. The wisdom of this posture was confirmed by both intellectual and religious conviction. Mr. Long View offered me a new l-o-n-g look at my journey toward inner wholeness."

The path of transformation can save us great pain. Often we struggle far too long with what can't be reworked but must be recast. Christian people often underestimate the extremely difficult process needed to change fundamental aspects of our behavior. Complex forces are behind everything we do. Rather than make the adjustments, many people simply become ill. Psychosomatic sickness may be an easier adjustment than realignment. For example, some people choose alcoholism or suicide to the basic change that might produce a new personhood. In contrast, transformation can lift us out of our quagmire by making the old issues irrelevant. Metamorphosis may be easier than stronger resolutions.

The Christian faith talks about the same possibility with such concepts as imputed righteousness and second birth. Scripture teaches some things can't be polished up; they have to be washed away. Unobtainable goodness is granted to us as a free gift of God's love. Our dreams often attempt to assist us in turning the doctrine into a fact.

As transformation occurs, many traits aren't changed as much as refocused. For example, anger can turn into the capacity to care passionately. Fear may become wise caution. Greed or covetousness is always insecurity waiting to be converted into trust. What is needed is a plunge into the pool of transformation.

Symbols of Transformation

Many images appear from time to time, setting the stage for transmutation. Perhaps two of the most mystifying and unexpected symbols of transformation are death and sexual encounters. Almost always these dreams are misunderstood, and the powerful force for good is missed. Here's the opportunity to find new insight. Let's start with the most intriguing and fascinating variety . . . those salacious sexual dreams.

Nighttime Escapades

Residue from our teenage years programs us to assume all sexual dreams are wish fulfillment. Often adults are scandalized, assuming an embarrassing fatal attraction to the person in the dream-world bedroom scenes. Periodically someone comes for counseling fearing he or she is about to be consumed by the lust exploding nightly in his or her dreams.

While occasionally the dream may represent the need for sexual release, more significant insight begins with the reminder that dream people are often symbolic representations of aspects of ourselves. Remember, the opposite sex is often our own Alter-Gender. You may want to go back to Chapter 5 and review the discussion of the content of the symbol.

We get an immediate idea what the dream is saying by looking very carefully at the Alter-Gender figure. Who is this person, and how do we know him or her? What is the context of our relationship? What do we like about this person? Dislike? Does this person attract us? What characteristics do we see in him or her?

The person in a sexual dream is often the Alter-Gender, full blown. We will possibly learn more about this portion of the Wilderness by looking at the sexual partner's real-life personality than through any other vehicle. Since Alter-Gender figures embody our idealized values, feelings, and hopes about the opposite sex, they are powerful symbols representing the female or male component in our own personalities.

Because we are fragmented, the feminine or masculine portions of our lives are neither complete nor integrated. One of our major lifetime tasks is to synthesize the opposite-gender side into the whole. One reason we select a particular mate is because this special person seems to embody all of the Alter-Gender data needed to make us whole. Unless we have a unique gift of celibacy or have reached an unusual state of personal development, we need someone of the opposite sex to complete our personhood. We are not weak as much as incomplete. In the marriage ritual, we proclaim "the two shall become as one," and that's exactly what we have in mind. These dreams present the hope for the end to our search for complete personhood.

Of course, our scheme is doomed to fail. No one person can bear the weight of what we must do for ourselves. Many marriages turn into a disappointment because one party illegitimately asks the other to be the source of his or her total fulfillment. However, separation isn't the solution either. Divorce is so painful because the Alter-Gender dimension is literally torn open. Wholeness leaves no alternative but to face up to the need to do our own inner work.

When the dream escapades appear, we need to study the partner very carefully. He or she was selected for reasons we may not be able to identify quickly, but one fact is clear. This one, particular individual embodies the essential components of the Alter-Gender. The more completely we understand what the person means to us, the clearer we will also be about why we are drawn to a certain type of person and what particularly attracts us. A client who was a pastor related the following dream to Paul Meier:

"A number of years ago a woman in my congregation kept appearing in sexual dreams. I was really mystified because she was such a virtuous person. However, in the dreams she took on the dimensions of a Hollywood siren. Because I admired her as a spiritual person and had no desire for any form of illicit relationships in my life, I couldn't understand the dreams. After a period of reflection I recognized she also had many traits of my own mother. She was intelligent, sensitive, perceptive, and . . . yes, physically attractive.

"She didn't work at being alluring; the quality was simply a natural part of who the woman was. Reluctantly I began to admit to myself just how sensual the woman *really* was.

"Slowly I began to understand the meaning of one of the most persistent archetypes in literature, poetry, and music. The saint-seductress symbol offers an almost irresistible allurement to men. Such persons embody great virtue and at the same time suggest a not-too-hidden promise of sexual adventure. Women understand this theme rather well when they buy perfumes entitled Passion, Obsession, or Secret Promise. Underneath the plain housedress lies the exotic lingerie."

This contradictory figure embodies one of the most difficult integration problems adults face. Men and women need to learn how to unify their religious and sexual dimensions in a way that honors both functions and yet keeps faith with personal values. Sexual dreams attempt to provide answers for the problem.

The pastor's sexual dreams about the woman in the church indicated that he was on the verge of working through this issue. His fantasy sexual union was in fact the inner integration of his own contrasting dimensions of virtue and sensuality. He was actually blending the fact that he is both a physical and spiritual entity, a sexual being and a praying person. The sexual act in the dream was the symbol of transformation as the two parts of him were becoming one.

The next time your mate talks aloud to another person in his or her dreams, don't get suspicious or worried. To the contrary, the spouse is probably defusing the problem of stray attractions!

A newlywed brought us a fascinating Alter-Gender dream with an unusual twist. The young woman dreamed she was in bed with her husband when the closet door flew open. There was Santa Claus watching them make love! Judy leaped out of bed, grabbed a pair of scissors, and started stabbing Kris Kringle! As the dream faded, she awoke in horror. Everything about the dream bothered the quite-proper young lady.

What would you say to Judy? Before you read further, take a moment and try to diagram the dream. Using the circumstances we have described, see if you can make some accurate projections about what is happening to the newlywed. Remember, no peeking for at least five minutes.

Ready to start again? Since we've told you Judy was recently married and implied her sexual life began with the marriage, we've already given you the context and the nature of the setting. The fact that the dream occurred in a bedroom also locates the place in her life where the action unfolded. Got the frame around the picture?

Let's think about Santa Claus for a moment. What does Santa symbolize? Wouldn't it be reasonable to see him as the person who rewards nice little girls for being good? He sure would be an inhibitor to letting go physically after a childhood of working to be worthy of gifts at Christmastime . . . particularly if you thought Santa might be peeking through the crack in the door!

With little prompting, Judy recognized that her new marital status required a major readjustment in how she viewed her own virtue. In a matter of minutes a religious service attempted to change Judy's orientation toward sexual activity from forbidden to being acceptable and encouraged. In her new relationship, she had to cease believing in being rewarded for chastity. The shift required putting a childhood dream to death! Santa had to go, even if violence was required.

Because the dream began with Judy in bed with her husband, the transformation function was implied in the setting. By calling Judy's attention to her struggle to free herself of childhood inhibitions, the dream helped her transform a little girl's reservations into an adult woman's privileges.

We don't have to be afraid of our sexual dreams, and we must not make hasty assumptions about their meaning. Often they come bearing symbols of transformation.

Doctor Death

Probably no dream can cause the degree of consternation that comes with a dream about death. While we have considered some premonition dreams, including Abraham Lincoln's discovery of a casket in the White House, the vast majority of such dreams are not about physical demise. These jolts of mortality signal a very important shift in a relationship, changes in perspective on some facet of past experience, or closure on some accomplishment in our own development. Each of these dreams attempts to help us leave behind an old aspect of behavior in favor of a new way.

Death dreams generally help us get ready for resurrection. Because they signal transformation, we can, in the most positive sense, call them visits from Doctor Death.

Many of the pagan funeral practices prevailing in our culture condition us to see death as the destroyer of all future possibility. Unfortunately, some churches have customs that only add to the problem. However, the Christian community has a message for the frightened world. Death has been transformed through the work completed on Easter morning! The enemy has become a servant.

Just as caterpillars metamorphose into butterflies, we recognize death as a new force for supreme transformation. Dreams of dying appropriate the resurrection message on behalf of our inner development. Let's consider several forms of visits from Doctor Death.

Encounters with the Deceased. The reappearance of a person six months to a year after his or her death is surprisingly common. The event may be so striking the dreamer is convinced he or she has been visited by someone returning from the other side. Again, we must remember the meaning of symbols. Dreams appear to confront us with areas of conflict begging resolution. One of Paul's clients told him:

"I was born shortly after my grandfather died. Much of the weight of family matters shifted to my mother. My grandmother also had her own special problems. During this time my mother struggled to know what to do with all of the responsibilities facing her. One night her father returned in a dream.

"'Eleanor,' Grandfather's voice called out of the dream, 'I'm here.' The old man walked in and sat down at the kitchen table. 'Whenever you need me, I will be here, child.' With that reassurance, Grandfather left once again.

"The following morning, the dream offered my mother continuing reassurance. She didn't really believe her father was literally there, but his memory imparted strength and reassurance. In a strange way, the dream also reassured her that she could let go of any lingering worry about him."

The reappearance of a lost relative usually is a signal to stop grieving for the person or at least to call our attention to the need to bring our sorrow to an end. No matter how close we were to the person, his or her death must not bring our lives to a halt. We can slide into a lingering, depressive grief and not even realize the condition. Generally the dream figure offers the promise of transformation of the mourning.

One of the most difficult issues to face is a hidden dread of letting the person go lest we be totally overwhelmed by grief. We may sense the hole in our life is so deep nothing can fill it. The possibility of nothingness is unbearable. We hang on to any vestige of the deceased as a hedge against the void. Under such circumstances the loved one may reappear to reassure us we can rebuild.

Unresolved grief may persist because of lingering discord not fully faced. Often these relationships were filled with conflicting emotion and contradictory feelings. Love-hate entanglements can wrap their ambivalence so tightly around our necks we have no idea how to get out of the noose. The emergence of the deceased may be an offer to help us cut the rope.

Such enigmatic dream figures present a need for extended conversations. We have previously described the technique of such written dialogues as a tour. Issues, worries, and unresolved problems inherited from these individuals during their lifetimes need to be and can be talked through.

Death of Public Figures.   What happens when you dream of the death of the president of the United States, the pope, or a famous movie star? You can bet 99.9 percent of the time nothing prophetic is going on!

If we look closely, we will discover the celebrity stands for ideals or values in our own lives. Generally he or she embodies qualities and characteristics we admire. The dream telegraphs a warning something is happening with these cherished values. Changes are afoot. We may be letting some dimension of our own lifestyles die.

Once again, a dialogue with the figure can be astonishingly revealing. A client of Paul Meier's had one of these remarkable dreams.

"During a strife-filled time in my own life, Abraham Lincoln appeared in a dream and began repairing my divided house. With hammer and nails, Abe boarded up the crack in the outside wall.

When he finished he turned toward me with advice: 'With malice toward none and charity toward all, we must be about the business of binding up the nation's wounds.' Then Abe left, and the dream ended.

"In my written dialogue with Lincoln about his instruction, I shifted to the chaotic situation in my own life. 'What should I do?' I asked. As my pencil flew across the paper, the unavoidable words formed: 'Can you forgive them?' While I wanted to argue that I had already forgiven, Abe knew I hadn't!"

Our Own Death. Time to check your last will and testament? Possibly, but not because of a dream portraying your own death. Remember, if the true self is to emerge, the Doorkeeper must release control! If the "I" in the dream is dying, wouldn't this be the Doorkeeper going down for the count? Sounds like good news!

Rejoice! Old motives and motivations are drying up. False identities and misplaced personas are being discarded. These dreams are the emotional fulfillment of the biblical injunction to deny ourselves, lay down our present lives, and pick up our crosses in order to find a new existence. We are being pushed toward the real and the authentic. Doctor Death has done his work well. The resurrection of the authentic self lies ahead.

Dreaming of our own death implies a newfound willingness to relinquish old roles, images, and relationships. We have found the higher path allowing us to transcend the unresolvable. Our many fragmented selves are coming into unity and singularity.

Your Assignment

Look back over your dream work to see if any symbols of transformation are there. Have you possibly overlooked some very important material with greater meaning than you might have previously thought? If you find such images, you will want to do the following exercise. If not, you may find other important dream personages you will want to pursue in a similar manner.

Re-enter the Wilderness just as if you were taking a tour. Once the mood is re-established, zero in on this one particular figure. Do everything possible to relate and understand what you are seeing. The task is to make this symbol as vivid and defined as possible.

Absorb the ambiance of the figure. Once the contact is as secure as possible, meditate on the significance of the person.

Envision walking around with a camcorder, taking in every inch from many different vantage points. Don't try to do anything more than absorb the essence of what is embodied before your inner eyes. Let the fullness of the figure emerge. You are not seeking a rational answer or an explanation. You are inviting transformation to go forward.

Like newlyweds consummating their love for each other, you are inviting the integration of the best in you to have full freedom for the work of metamorphosis to be completed.

You will want to pray at the end of the experience for truly you are about the work of God.

Chapter 12

PUMP
PRIMERS

Tips for Interpretation

Even a relatively stupid feeling out of one's own
images is better than reason or the guess of the best
outside experts. Outsiders are inclined to project
their own lives into one's own images. . . . But you
are the life that projects your images. Your most
halting understanding is closer to its own source.
WILSON VAN DUSEN, *THE NATURAL DEPTH IN MAN*

The world of dreamscapes is too vast to be covered by one book, a library, or a lifetime of investigation. What counts is not reaching a goal but staying on the journey. The only truly worthwhile objective is coming to personal wholeness and maturity. With this aim in mind, we want to give you a potpourri of additional tips—we call them pump primers—to help you broaden your insights.

Dream travelers need all the help they can get reading the signs along the way. Since no one can fully or accurately read anyone else's dream mail, the best we can do is walk alongside helping the neophyte recognize what the untrained eye is likely to miss. However, in every incidence, we have to be our own interpreters. We hope our insights have led to the creation of our own special set of guidelines and personal perceptions.

Understanding dreams requires a difficult paradigm shift. Most people struggle in switching from rational to symbolic thinking. Their usual patterns of syllogistic logic have to be set aside for intuitive thinking. We don't learn to do dream work as much as we "get the hang" of how it's done. The dreams we've shared and dissected are meant to help you *feel* your way into the process.

Just as working with clay allows your hands to express what's waiting to come out, dreamscapes have to be unleashed and released. They can't be attacked and dissected like cutting up frogs. By this point, we hope you've slipped into this new way of looking at dreams, people, and things. Like an artist, you've discovered how to find the inner essence, the ultimate meaning behind what the eye beholds. Form has given way to substance.

If so, you've probably discovered dream experiences and processes that are somewhat different from what we've been describing. Good. Images and patterns have possibly surfaced that vary from anything covered thus far. Excellent! You're launching your own private safaris into parts of your Wilderness.

Here's some more insight to help the expedition succeed.

Multi-Levels

This tip was discovered only after hours of stumbling in the dark. Dreams may often consist of several tiers. Each layer will have its own meaning and significance. Since we are solving a mystery, not an algebra problem, we should be prepared to make several trips around some symbols, expecting to see something different each time.

Paul Meier had such a dream with fascinating implications,

even though the intense nightmare left him quite shaken. His notes reflect this chain of events.

"I was on a vacation with my sons, staying in a cabin on a hill overlooking a California-style freeway. The highway was packed with fast-moving cars. Suddenly, one car stopped and another ran into the back of it. The pileup was on! Abruptly a fire truck pulling a storage trailer plowed into the entanglement. However, instead of ramming the cars, the fire truck flew over the top like a cartoon vehicle. Next a Mack truck double the size of a normal eighteen-wheeler came flying in but tried to avoid the pileup by going around the side. Twenty-one cars were wrecked. I tried to dial 911 for help, and I knew my boys and I should go down to work with the injured, but I was afraid to face the terrible pain and suffering.

"I awoke struggling to know how to respond to this terrible problem. The next morning I couldn't decide what to do for a while. I thought maybe I should call all of my six children and warn them to be careful on the highway. After reflection, I decided maybe I was just getting carried away with the dream-book project and let the whole thing go. I *did* pray for the safety of my family."

Paul didn't have time to work on the dream right then; he took off for work. Then a remarkable series of coincidences followed. The memory of the dream caused him to drive more cautiously than usual, but that afternoon Paul had significant car trouble. While crossing a railroad track, the car began swaying violently because a bearing had gone out.

The same afternoon, his daughter Cheryl called from California to report her own car wreck. The brakes had gone out on the Meier car, causing Cheryl to skid into the next lane. The car following behind crashed into the back of her car, totaling the vehicle. Cheryl walked away unharmed, but the unusual chain of car accidents was hard to write off as coincidental. Two days later, Paul's son had a similar car accident. And a few weeks later, another son totaled his car but was unharmed. Paul had to take a long second look at the dream.

What did Paul experience? A nightmare? A prophetic dream? Subjective meaning? How would you treat the experience?

Paul went back to the dream looking for the larger significance; he began studying a number of details. He remembered that a few days prior to the dream, a friend had died in a car wreck. At the time of the accident, the friend was embroiled in marital difficulties. The loss was still heavy in Paul's mind. In addition, the number twenty-one rang a bell. Paul's novel, *The Third Millennium,* deals with the twenty-one judgments in the book of Revelation.[1] Twenty-one was a good way for Paul to express disaster and judgment.

When Paul realized the dream had come at a time when he was acutely in touch with the needs of other people, the context of the dream became clearer.

The highway was Paul's symbolic metaphor for the world. Multitudes of people go whizzing by day after day, blind to the disasters just ahead. With no awareness of the value of their lives, throngs of the misguided speed on toward their rendezvous with pain and death. Cars without safety controls, this modern image of sheep without a shepherd touched Paul deeply. He wanted to leap into the flow of traffic and stop the rush toward madness and destruction.

Like a fire engine speeding to stop an impending disaster, Paul wanted to tell the drivers, "Slow down and smell the roses. Come on up the hill and take a vacation with me. Get a new perspective."

At that point, a meaning for the end of the dream surfaced. While he identified with the hurting people, Paul wasn't sure if he really had the energy to get into the fray. He was struggling with both the call for help and his own apprehension about the demands placed on his life. Paul felt the pain of observing hurting people while being pulled apart by the limitations of his personal capacity to help.

Yet something more was going on in the dream. Another level was moving beneath the first explanation. Paul slowly recognized he was caught in the middle of the freeway jam. He was also viewing the pain of his own entanglement in the human rat race.

Unfortunately, the practice of psychiatry involves more than quietly talking with and listening to people. The highly involved world of the sixty-five Minirth Meier New Life Clinics, including radio and television programming, has pressing demands. He often found himself dragging a "truckload" of baggage into the marketplace. Paul's attempts to carry on a meaningful ministry to people was getting rear-ended by the unceasing demands pouring in upon him every day!

The dream suggested Paul needed a higher perspective on where his life was going. Paul should take a *vacation* from the unrelenting pace and find a place to look down on the current situation in his own world.

An alternative meaning to the end of the dream surfaced. Paul was trapped in his own ambivalence over what to do with the freeway-style gridlock in his own professional world. He wanted to help people but was having a hard time getting through the pileup in his business life. These unresolved issues felt like a disaster.

Which set of conclusions is the correct interpretation? What solution is accurate? Good news. You don't have to pick one. They are all valid.

On one level the dream warned of car trouble. Sure enough, car trouble followed. Another level called attention to a troubled state of mind. Paul needed to sort out his own feelings about the demands being placed on his life. However, at another level he also needed to address collisions at the office.

Obviously, the dream was not a typical nightmare or a prophetic dream. Still, each dimension was there. The subjective elements were the strongest part of the dream, but the conflict was strong enough to make the experience feel like a night terror. Such a dream reminds us how complex the dream world can be. And how powerfully helpful!

The Jigsaw Puzzle

Often we get confused when we get a piece of one dream layer misplaced or intertwined with a fragment from another level. When we hit a roadblock, we should consider the possibility of misguided jumping back and forth between layers without awareness of the juxtaposition of material.

The same phenomenon occurs in great books. Hemingway's *The Old Man and the Sea,* Steinbeck's *The Bear,* or Melville's *Moby Dick* are stories of multiple strata. One dimension describes a person's odyssey while another theme in the same story is a representation of universal conflict or the ongoing human struggle with nature. The fullest comprehension of the complete story demands awareness of all of these levels, but it is important to keep them separate as we read the book.

The following diagram will help clarify some possibilities in dream interpretation. We've drawn a picture of what the different levels might look like if they were laid out like a succession of events in the plot in a story. Numbers represent the symbols in the dream as they appear in sequence. Each level is a complete layer of meaning and a total dream story within itself.

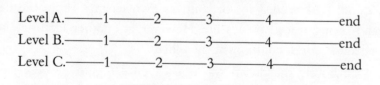

```
Level A.——1———2———3———4————end
Level B.——1———2———3———4————end
Level C.——1———2———3———4————end
```

Confusion results if we get one piece of one level into the story line of another layer. The distorted arrangement might look like:

Level A.——1——(Level B. 2)——3——(Level C. 4)——5

Even though our understanding of symbol 2 in level B might be correct, imposition into level A would distort our understanding the dreamscape of that particular level. Obviously, the mixing of the levels could only result in confusion and make it difficult to see the full meaning of each level. One part may be accurately understood, but the total picture will be distorted.

We must start over and slowly get back in sync with each level. The mixing of layers is often the reason why, several hours later after we've failed to make sense out of the dream, everything falls into place. The unconscious mind has its own way of reassembling the pieces in proper order. Many times we need to live with a dream for several days, letting it roll over and over in our minds until we've thoroughly absorbed the ambiance of the symbols.

Advanced students of dream work will begin to develop an awareness of the interconnectedness of all dreamscapes. Initially, individual dreams seem to be quite random, sailing in out of the blue. Each night's production feels quite independent of the previous night. With time and work we will come to see the big picture. Each piece is a part of a much larger whole.

Dreams don't connect in a consecutive arrangement. Rather, they are like the order of the planets in our solar system, circling around the sun. For centuries astronomers made many miscalculations about the structure of the solar system because they didn't have a comprehensive perspective. Only after discovering the centrality of the sun did the nature of the heavenly order fall into place. In exactly the same way, we must identify the central issues, the Tornadoes, the blocks to integration, before we fully recognize the order in the dream world.

The dream constellations look something like the following:

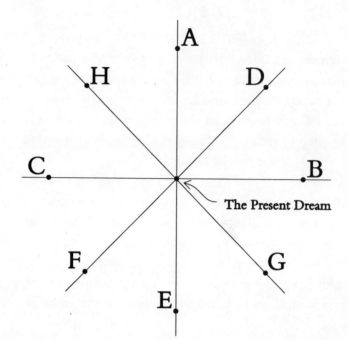

The key tip is to remember dreams don't follow the rational logic of daylight. Stay with the paradoxical reasoning of your inner world, and don't try to force the dreams into preconceived molds.

Remakes

Have you noticed how often Hollywood recasts classic movies? Every so many years we get the updated version of *Miracle on 34th Street* or a thriller like *Cape Fear*. Sometimes an old story like *The Phantom of the Opera* is retold with a complete, modern rebuilding of the setting or the costumes. Same story, different shape.

The longer you work with dreams, the more aware you will become of this same phenomenon. In the middle of solving a dream puzzle you will suddenly realize, "Good heavens! I worked on this same story line two months ago!" Through the years you'll be surprised at how creative the remakes can be.

Why the basic story in a remake?

The tip: *Dreams don't appear to tell what we already know.* They appear to inform us of information we're not processing. The problem is we are either not getting the point, or we're not acting on the message. The Doorkeeper hasn't allowed the communiqué from the Wilderness to get through.

For example, let's take another look at Robert Wise's dreams of attack. He said, "I went back to my dream journey and started running down the various forms this type of dream took. In looking at the interconnectedness, I learned something I had never seen in the individual parts.

"First, I found a dream from nearly ten years earlier involving a shootout with the police. In the dream I'm watching a gunfight in which, oddly enough, no one is actually killed. When the dream ends, all the attackers come out for a party, as if the fight was only part of a play or a rehearsal.

"The next attack dream came on April 15, income tax day. An appropriate time for assault experiences! I am in my home with my wife and children when I discover a terrorist assault is under way. Disguised as college boys, the terrorists are after my computer and electrical paraphernalia. Because I also have on a disguise, I'm able to escape."

A review of several years' material produced the same story in other forms. A review of the entire series took Robert to a surprising new place of insight. He knew people organize their lives around a few basic emotional issues such as anger, guilt, fear, worry. He was not sure what his basic issue was, but he knew it certainly couldn't be fear! Most of his life he'd been something of a daredevil, unafraid to try anything at least once. Robert was known for dancing on the edge of the sword. However, the review of attack dreams gave him quite a surprise!

"The chase dreams called my bluff! Much to my consternation, I was forced to discover that fear *was* the basic issue in the center of the Wilderness. The whole picture taught me more than I could have learned from any of the parts.

"My defiant attitude was an inner defense against the fact of my fear. In each of the dreams, the attackers were trying to get me to face up to the bottom line. I couldn't be a whole person until I faced my own inner fear. The attackers were also trying to get me to see my learned reaction to fearful situations. Fear caused me to put up a Promethean defense of myself. As a matter of fact, I would go to unintelligent extremes to protect myself when fear was involved. I had learned to depend on no one but myself under these circumstances. The attackers were also calling my attention to the isolation fear created."

Take a tip: If the remakes appear, you're missing something in the basic message. Look again.

Another tip: *When an interpretation of a dream leaves us unmoved or disappointed, we've missed the meaning.* In looking at the remakes, you will probably find your original deciphering left you with a "what-the-heck" or "no-big-deal" attitude. If so, you haven't gotten the point yet. Keep working until you come to a satisfying sense of important insight.

S-t-r-a-n-g-e Symbols

Here's the tip: *Don't panic when the symbol is just too far-out for comfort.* And don't switch from the methods of interpreting symbols offered in the previous chapters!

Often we come to unusual dreams so loaded with emotional significance we are sure we've stumbled on to a completely new type of entity. Rather than shifting gears, we need to stay with the principles outlined in the previous chapters.

Here are some of the more bizarre forms that often hang people up.

Many people worry about encountering some demonic force if they pursue dream work. Along the way they hear of someone dreaming of the devil, and their worst fears are confirmed. What does it mean to dream about talking to the devil?

While the earliest Christians of the first five centuries wrote a great deal about the significance of encountering God in dreams, they wrote virtually nothing about meeting the devil. Centuries of dream work infer such confrontations are very rare.

Our tip: *Satanic representations should be dealt with like all other symbols.* Rather than meeting a real creature, the depiction generally embodies some aspect of ourselves. The issue isn't whether we have met the real devil but where the "ole devil" is living in us.

The great Italian violinist Giuseppe Tartini had an experience that illustrates this point. Feeling a great surge of inspiration, Tartini began composing a sonata. Near the end of the piece, he lost direction and couldn't finish his composition. Of course, Tartini was quite frustrated. He took a nap and ended up in an important dream. As Tartini wandered across a barren and empty dreamscape, he came upon the devil. In return for his soul, the devil offered to complete the composition. Tartini agreed, and the devil picked up a violin and began playing. The violinist awoke with strains of the magnificent finale ringing in his ear. He quickly completed what he called "The Devil's Sonata."[2]

On the basis of what you've learned to date, what suggestion would you offer Tartini if he came to you for help? Before you read further, lay down your book and reflect for a minute. Of all the People Paradigm symbols we've discussed so far, do any fit the violinist's encounter with the devil? Again, no fair peeking until you've worked on the problem.

Ready to start again? Did you consider using the dream aspect that embodies qualities we haven't become comfortable with or would like to negate? Remember the Shadow we discussed in Chapter 5?

Creativity arises from the Shadow portion of the Wilderness. Every artist knows the truism that pain is the parent of ingenuity. Attempts to work through childhood suffering bestow on us a rare, compensating gift of originality. At the same time, these early difficult experiences are the stuff we most want to forget and to jettison. Inner unresolved tension produces many a gifted but troubled artist. When we run into this area, we often feel as if we're doing business with the devil. We must take a long second look.

We could safely suggest to Giuseppe that he had met the Shadow dressed up in a Halloween costume. He could dialogue with this figure just as he could with any other dream symbol and gain further insight into the meaning of the dream as well as a part of his life he tried to deny. Unlocking the Shadow offers great reserves of inspiration.

On the other hand, evil is a reality and can occur in dreams. Demonic encounters are especially powerful, disturbing dreams. We are left unraveled, disconcerted, sure we have faced the dragon. When we strongly feel such an encounter may have occurred, we will probably want to seek help from a biblical spiritual director or a biblical counselor who takes this realm seriously. We do best to work through the dream with a competent guide.

Should we be concerned for demonic infiltration? Tertullian, the ancient Church Father, believed dreams have three sources: our fears and anxieties, revelation from God, and temptation from Satan. Tertullian certainly recognized the possibility of evil influence. We always do well to be aware of the possibilities of seduction. But how shall we recognize deception?

Direct encounter with evil is not unlike confrontations with the Divine. These numinous experiences are so overpowering there is no question of the context. However, direct experience with evil is frightening and fortunately extremely rare. You will know when you have seen the enemy.

How about the more subtle influence of infiltration? As we have already pointed out a number of times, dreams have to be tested by an objective standard. In and of themselves, they do not constitute an objective canon of truth. Scripture is essential for clarification. In addition, the personality and spirit of Jesus the Christ is the only appropriate winnowing rod to sort out spiritual direction. Any suggestion or direction contrary to the personality of Jesus is to be immediately rejected. Dreams are no different from motivations, inspirations, and ideas arising from prayer or contemplation. The issue isn't what feels good but what *is* good.

However, like all symbols, evil usually comes in an oblique and disguised form. Generally when the demonic appears, we can expect the symbols to be less obvious and explicit than costumes worn at Halloween. Herman Riffel, a Baptist minister and professional counselor, is also a student of dreams. While working in the mission fields around the world, he often encountered this dimension. In his book *Your Dreams: God's Neglected Gift,* he describes a number of these occurrences. An African pastor brought him this dream:

"I was in my village trying to reach out for God, but I could not get through to Him because some little men were hindering me," the pastor said. "All my efforts to break through to God were of no avail. Then, strangely, a ladder was set up for me, and by the use of that ladder, I was able to reach God."[3]

Herman's first impulse was to assume the dream was about pygmies, but he knew too much about interpretation to accept such a rational answer. He pushed on to discover the meaning of "little people" in African culture. At the next village Herman discovered a two-foot hut built for the "little men." To his amazement, he found the place was reserved for the spirits of the dead! Witchcraft offerings were made at the door of the hut to appease these spirits.

Remembering the symbol of the ladder in Jacob's dream at Bethel, Herman was able to put the rest of the dream pieces in place. The ladder was a clear symbol of the power of God to prevail over the intrusion of evil. The African pastor quickly recognized he had allowed the prevailing satanic witchcraft of the area to hinder his prayers. The pastor came to grips with the power of the cross to defeat Satan in all his works and ways. The matter was quickly ended.

Such experiences do happen but should not hinder our dream work. First, ignoring the dream *won't* make it go away. The dream is a friend sounding the warning. The dream calls our attention to something we've missed. Second, while evil may intrude, dreams remain a gift from God. As is true with all encounters with evil, we simply evoke the superiority and total sufficiency of the finished work of Christ on the cross as the victory over all demonic intrusions. The matter is finished.

Nudity

Ever have one of those, "I dreamed I walked down Fifth Avenue in my Maidenform bra" experiences? It does tend to leave one rather undone.

Our tip: *Look at the feeling created by the dream.* Did you awake embarrassed or exhilarated? Did the dream leave you worried or encouraged? The feeling often tells us whether the dream is subjective or objective.

Objective nudity dreams seem to be rather factual and leave us unmoved. They may be calling our attention to a very practical problem. Something may literally be wrong with our clothes. For example, we might be preparing for a trip and leaving our pants behind! Is a strategically located zipper about to go? The movie producer has a unique set of eyes.

On the other hand, nudity dreams are more likely to be subjective. The context of such dreams offers the clue. The dreamer is at a party or the office with a group of people when the person realizes his or her pants are missing. While the dreamer is horrified, no one else in the crowd seems to notice. Many people experience this particular scenario as a recurring dream.

Don't worry! You're not an exhibitionist waiting to come out of the closet.

The Wilderness issue may be fear of exposure as an incompetent or inadequate person. We may be afraid of being placed in a vulnerable position. The context of the dream suggests a concern for being caught "with our pants down." Surely everyone can identify with the apprehension of being made to look incompetent.

However, the dream offers reassurance. Other people aren't worried. The indifference of the people in the dream is a hint we are placing too great an emphasis on adequacy.

On another level, nudity dreams may indicate a desire for greater honesty or openness. The nonchalance of the dream crowd offers encouragement to feel safe in revealing more about ourselves.

Telephone Dreams

Did you ever wake up to a telephone ringing, only to discover no one's on the line? You were hearing the dream line! It can sure ruin a good night's sleep.

The dream is literally trying to get us to wake up, to pay attention. We are missing an important message from the call-waiting portion of the dream world. We need to look for a lack of awareness of what previous dreams have been saying.

A similar meaning is found in dreams about telephone calls that

211

won't go through. The warning may be about a breakdown in communication with others. We need to immediately explore our "connections" with the important people in our lives.

When the call is to a specific person, we may want to explore the implications of not being able to get that person's "number." Much to our surprise, we may discover something deceptive is working behind the scenes of this relationship. In a similar vein, disruptions in the dreamscape's phone network may offer clues about secret saboteurs affecting our connectedness. The sabotage may be coming from within or from people we know. Either way, phone dreams are generally "wake-up calls."

Losing Valuables

Our tip: *Start on the objective level. Ask yourself, am I about to lose something of worth?* Dreams offer an amazing wealth of intuitive insight. Many times we are so preoccupied with our pressing demands we miss a vital aspect of daily business happening right under our noses. We may be letting important issues slip through our fingers.

Several years ago Robert Wise was in a casual conversation with the church's business manager. Dorothy laughed and related a strange dream she'd had the night before. She dreamed her computer lost all the material. She casually noted it was important to be more diligent in backing up the entries. Two days later Dorothy lost a month's work that wasn't backed up!

Once we're satisfied we have our eyes open, we can turn to the possibility of a subjective metaphoric meaning. Our tip: *Ask yourself if any personal values are in danger of being lost.* You will want to examine the lost object carefully as a symbolic representation of personal standards or ideals. Integrity may be slipping away. The chances are high you aren't in touch with compromises you are making.

On the other hand, the dream may be suggesting the need to

jettison an old portion of your life. Growth may demand your letting go of a part of the past. Inadequate values must often be discarded for maturity to emerge.

Let's look at the other side of the coin. What about dreams of finding something of worth? Our tip: *Look carefully at the amount discovered and where you located the treasure.*

Since numbers are important clues, we always wrestle with whether a figure represents an actual amount, an idea, or a date on the calendar. Many times a number suggests our age when a particularly important event occurred in our personal history. In the same way, the location of the valuable find is filled with clues about meaning.

On the subjective side, discovery dreams point us toward inner treasure we may need to appropriate. When life is tough and we're feeling depleted, the dream can help us find a new storehouse of resources. Our tip: *Look for inner riches you didn't know you had.*

Missing the Boat

Who hasn't gone to bed worrying about waking up in time to catch an early flight? All night long you keep waking up with the strange premonition the alarm should have gone off. Overly objective concern is a pain in the neck!

On a more emotional level, such dreams ought to be looked at carefully as metaphors. Is it possible some plan, some goal, something in our lives is slipping away like a lost opportunity? The dream may be telling us to take a second look at our life strategy.

Our tip: *Explore how the dream makes you feel.* Are you left with regret? Remorse? As an exercise in exploring the meaning of the symbol, you might want to fantasize going ahead and boarding the plane, letting the craft take you where it will. At the end of the flight you'll be clear about the destination you were about to overlook.

More Tips for Dream Travelers

Pump primers help stimulate your imagination. They are not intended to be a collection of solutions. Each of these tips is offered only as a stimulus to your own inner explorations. Remember, no one can tell you dogmatically what your symbols mean. The answers are found only in your personal dreamland.

In order to help you further explore the meaning of how your personal movie producer puts dreams together, a glossary of common symbols is included in the appendix. Remember, these are only indicators—suggestions—and are not intended to be taken literally. They should not be applied to someone else's dream as if to predict meaning. Use them to help you find clues, but don't build any monuments on these building blocks.

Your Assignment

Your pump should be primed and the flow of meaning ready to spill over. Each morning you can awaken to a bucket filled with new, fresh meaning and insight for living. You have found one of God's most valuable tools and gifts. You are a very fortunate person.

Your assignment? Spend the rest of your life enjoying the mysteries of the night. Become the best possible companion to your dream friends and learn to accept every favor they offer. Develop your dream notebook into such a volume of material you will become the absolute unparalleled authority on yourself. Good things are ahead.

Happy dream trails.

Chapter 13

ENCOURAGEMENT
The Journey Is Enough

The problem of the second half of life is to find a new meaning and purpose in living, and this, perhaps strangely enough, is best found in the neglected, inferior, and underdeveloped side of the personality. Many people, however, cannot face such a possibility, and prefer to cling to values of youth, and even pursue them in an exaggerated fashion; for them the concept of individuation can have no meaning.

FRIEDA FORHAM, AN INTRODUCTION TO JUNG'S PSYCHOLOGY

While helping complete the editing of the manuscript for this book, Bob and Retha Bierschank studied each chapter carefully. They quickly got the hang of applying the People Paradigm and became quite adept in deciphering dream symbols.

Near the end of the project their sixteen-year-old grandson came for a visit. During the night Jonathan had a disturbing dream.

Voices in the dream suggested Jonathan might not make it to age seventeen. The young man perceived a warning of impending death. One single phrase rolled around and around through his sleep: *"No seventeen!"*

As the dream came to an end, someone handed him a slip with the message "N O 1 7." However, Jonathan received the page upside down. As he looked at the topsy-turvy message, he saw "L I O N." He awoke in consternation that the warning "N O 17" had turned into the name of an animal. (Try turning the message upside down.)

When Jonathan shared his consternation with his grandmother, she was able to help him understand this unusual experience. The heart of the dream was Jonathan's quite normal apprehension about growing up. He really wasn't sure becoming seventeen was so terribly inviting. Thundering in Jonathan's Wilderness was considerable doubt about his capacity to meet the demands of adulthood. Nevertheless, the dream offered him profound reassurance, similar to Simba's discovery in the story of *The Lion King.* Waiting in Jonathan's shadow was lion power!

The never-ending creative capacities of the unconscious are a marvel to behold. Such amazing and extraordinary experiences are enough to make dream work worthwhile. If for no other reason, understanding each of these wonderful mysteries of the night is enough to justify the trip.

But, of course, there is so much more.

Keep On Truckin'

We hope this book has helped you create a new habit; we hope you've made dream work a permanent part of your life. Certainly the stories and anecdotes are fascinating. Everyone is intrigued with the bizarre imagery of the dreamscape. But sharing dream tales won't change anyone or anything. You have to do the work for yourself day after day, week after week, if your dreams are going to accomplish their purpose.

Why should you pay the price in time and effort? Here are three major reasons: transformation, discernment, and growth.

1. Transformation

During the first few years of Robert Wise's ministry, a parishioner confronted him with her misgivings. "I've heard all the talk and the preaching," the young woman said. "But does anyone really change? Is anyone truly different because of what he or she believes?" Jan crossed her arms and raised her eyebrows.

Sure, Robert knew values and beliefs are changed through faith. Many people do clean up their acts, and multitudes develop a new sense of relationship with God. But the woman wanted to know something that was not so easy to affirm: When it's all said and done, are church people more loving and kinder because of what they believe? Do personalities modify? Can old fears dissolve and egotism diminish with time? Are people still changed in the ways talked about in the New Testament?

The question stuck. As the years went by, Robert was haunted by the implications of Jan's inquiry. He watched denominational leaders in power struggles fight with the same fierceness as political parties locked in mortal combat over a national election. Church splits and wars demonstrated mean-spiritedness exceeding anything normally found in the business world. Bible-quoting members were capable of spreading malicious gossip, attacking each other's characters, and attempting to destroy people with whom they disagreed. The contradiction between what many Christians affirm and do has long been a well-known national scandal.

Years later the young woman's question remained relevant. Why don't people change more? How can people go to worship services and Bible studies decade after decade and not be different?

Robert discovered the answer is frighteningly simple. Believers put on beliefs and ideas like adding a sweater, a coat, another layer of clothing to what they are already wearing. They seldom stand naked before God to receive new skin. Too many people never allow their convictions to penetrate their souls and bring genuine wholeness. They are afraid to allow the truth to confront perceptions of themselves, revealing basic fears, infantile needs, and prejudices. Faith is only a rational system that does not settle beneath the level of logic. In short, regardless of what they say they believe, these people have either lost or never found their souls.

Churches are filled with people who believe the Christian faith has great power. Many just don't know yet what it is and haven't yet experienced the difference it can make.

Dream work can change this quagmire. Dreams offer windows to the soul. They take us far beyond the world of logic. Listening to their messages is one of the most effective ways possible to hear the sounds of the heart. Anyone seeking to be more consistent, honest, lucid, and transparent will find dreams to be a most valuable tool for transformation. They offer the mechanism for change. Dreams *can* help release the power in our faith.

Dream work offers you great possibility for creative and constructive change.

2. Discernment

And why is genuine, redemptive change so unusual? Why do we add another layer of veneer instead of paying the price for a completely new surface? Too often the fear of the truth lurking in our shadow stifles our quest for authenticity. This issue is particularly difficult for religious people with legalistic tendencies.

A psychiatrist, not a theologian, wrote:

The great events of our world as planned and executed by

man do not breathe the spirit of Christianity but rather of un-
adorned paganism. . . . Christian education has done all that is
humanly possible, but it has not been enough. Too few people
have experienced the divine image as the inner-most possession of their own souls. Christ only meets them from without,
never from within the soul; this is why dark paganism still
reigns there, a paganism which, now in a form so blatant that
it can no longer be denied and now, in all too threadbare disguise, is swamping the world of so-called Christian culture.[1]

Dream trips into the Wilderness can dramatically change this
condition in yourself. Insight is a natural by-product of discovering
the truth about who you are. These encounters save you from the
painful habit and deadly error of doing the opposite of what you
profess.

One of the dictums of dream work is, "If you don't deal with
your Shadow, it will deal with you." Ignoring inner issues will not
make them go away. Many an affair, bout of depression, or breakdown is the result of ignoring the Shadow! At the very least the
result is projections aimed at others with laser-beam precision.

What was the source of the Salem witch-hunts? What produced the character assassinations of the McCarthy era? Why can
seemingly loving Christian people turn on each other with the
vengeance of man-eating tigers? Hate, suspicion, paranoid distrust,
gossip—the viciousness of accusers lurks in their own souls like a
hidden terrible infection, a psychological time bomb poised to
explode. When the right target crosses their paths, a volcanic erup-
tion follows. There is no discernment.

*Consistent dream work offers you the possibility of lancing the festering
boil in the Shadow, cleansing the forgotten wounds of the past, and releasing
the unrecognized hate from old prejudices. You are able to get well before you
make somebody else sick.*

3. Growth

Could there be a much more frightening fate than to realize just moments before your death that you had lived your entire life as someone else? You missed being uniquely who you were! After your life is finished, you will not be asked why you were not the apostle Paul, Saint Francis, Mother Teresa, Martin Luther King, Jr., or Billy Graham. You will be asked why you weren't you.

Growth in virtue is not possible unless there is a corresponding growth in authenticity. The issue is self-consistency, individuation. Because we don't have eyes in the back of our heads, a dimension of our personhood is always hidden from us. If the matter is left there, we inevitably are limited in what we can achieve. For this reason, dream work is a must for anyone concerned with genuineness, veracity, and maturity.

We live in an age that mistakes data for meaning, busyness for purpose, and accumulation for class. Periodically we must remind ourselves that a computer will never be capable of maturation. Knowledge without insight is of limited value. Authentic growth is impossible without integration of experience. Dreams offer the highest possible platforms from which we can view our life adventures and turn experience into wisdom.

Few pursuits can facilitate personal growth as effective as consistent, persistent dream work.

During Paul Meier's psychiatric residency, he was under constant examination. After an hour of working with a client, Paul would spend an hour with a therapist analyzing his reaction to the patient. Every day was filled with trips into his unconscious world. In order to develop insight into his patients, Paul was constantly probing his own childhood memories. During this time, he had an intense unique dream.

Paul began a chronologically backward journey through the events of his life as if it were a movie running in reverse. The amazing dream trip began with his psychiatric residency, went into childhood, and eventually continued all the way back into his mother's womb. As he later worked on the dream, one particular event stood out. Four-year-old Paul was lying on the dining room floor writing his name and "1949" on the bottom of a dining-room chair. After he tired of writing, Paul constructed a hideout around the chair with blankets and entertained himself playing a game under the quilts.

The next day, Paul talked to his mother to check on the accuracy of the dream events. Mrs. Meier especially remembered his chair story and confirmed the details. Paul concluded the dream had come to help him develop his abilities to be a psychiatrist. Memories long lost in his memory banks had been evoked with incredible precision. Paul had no question of the ability of dreams to provide the material for growth.

Are you completely convinced yet? Our hope is you will not finish this book without having developed a commitment to pursue the dream style of life. *But you must pursue a discipline.* Your efforts will be more than rewarded.

You don't have to prove anything. Just the journey will be enough.

You Can Go Home Again

Who does not long for the recovery of the rose-colored images of yesterday? While playwrights and novelists have settled the possibility of ever going back to the place where we literally left off, dream work allows us to deal with the unfinished business back home. The neurotic need to reclaim what never was can be laid to rest through dream work. In the healthiest sense of the phrase, our dreams will take us home again.

Perhaps you've wondered whatever became of Robert's abandonment dream. Throughout the book, we've explored various dimensions that surfaced as the dream was considered and worked on over the years. Each discovery of meaning was helpful and brought needed insight, but something was always missing. The dream continued for years as a Tornado in the Wilderness.

While Robert always knew he was adopted, the experience was surrounded by impenetrable mystery. Feelings, images, and memories floated in and out. Even as a small child, he could not decide what was fantasy and fact. Because he did not bond well with his adoptive family, the problem only increased with time. The recurring dream would not go away.

In the darkest nights, the cotton field dreamscape would reappear, the tall green-and-brown stalks shaking in the hot wind. The child would discover workers loading up in the truck at the far end of the field. Terror at the possibility of being left sent the small boy running as fast as his little legs could carry him. As always, Robert tripped and fell into the sandy soil. Far away, the truck roared to life, and the tailgate slammed shut.

As his mother disappeared in a cloud of dust, Robert was swept away by a flood of terror. Each time the dreamscape ended with the child left alone in the field, tears running down his face. Abandoned.

The dream did not change with the passing years.

Finally, Robert decided to do everything necessary to find where the dream originated. After searching through all the personal documents available to him, he started a legal quest to find his original birth certificate. Through the clandestine work of a friend, the legal fragments of the puzzle slowly fell into place. Much to his surprise, Robert discovered his original name had been Edlow Moses. The pieces were beginning to come together.

Although Robert's father had died ten years earlier, his biological mother was still living in a little town in Alabama. On a cold, early-spring morning, Robert flew to Atlanta and then drove to

Roanoke. The ninety-mile trip seemed like an eternity but as the miles clicked past, the journey felt more like an excursion through a time tunnel. Years of wondering, worrying, and pondering drifted across his mind as he recognized how this one dream had been a dynamic shaping influence in his life. Whatever loss the experience represented, the dream had more than compensated for the deficit by creating sensitivities, awareness, and opening inner doors that would have gone unnoticed save for this one dreamscape.

Following the little map his mother sent, Robert wound his way through the streets lined with pines and magnolias until he spotted the address. A little white-haired lady sat rocking on the front porch as if she had waited in that one spot for forty years. For many years she too had carried her own dream in her heart.

Even though the next few hours seemed like a blur, Robert could feel the broken chunks of the past coming together like a priceless vase being mended. Ghosts from the past evaporated in the light of day as his mother filled in the missing blanks. Frightening family circumstances and the unfolding drama of World War II had sent him into his private exile. The parties making the arrangements had promised a reunion at a later time, but they had lied. They had all been betrayed by the best of intentions.

After their first supper together in more than forty years, Robert and his mother gathered beside the fireplace for dessert. His mother said, "I can still see that last night as if it were yesterday. I held you up above my head and looked in your eyes. I said, 'Come back to me, little boy, come back to me.' I prayed to God it would be done. And I prayed every day of my life for it yet to be. And now, it is so."

And then the dreamscape was clear. In a strange way Robert could never have known cognizantly, the dream was a symbolic picture of the rupture in the bonding established so many years before. The trauma of his childhood was encapsulated in a dream that was so vivid it was nearly impossible to distinguish from the event itself.

The years following that night were extremely rich for mother and son. Their relationship became deeply fulfilling. During the last weeks of her life, Robert stayed with his mother in a hospital room in Montgomery. When she finally slipped away, Robert sat alone holding her hand, grateful to have been her final comfort.

The journey had been quite enough.

MORE PUMP
PRIMERS
𝒜 Dictionary of Symbols

*I have had a dream, past the wit of a man to say
what dream it was.*
SHAKESPEARE, *A MIDSUMMER NIGHT'S DREAM*

All dream symbols are particular to the dreamer. No one can tell another person what his or her images mean. Advice must be pondered and confirmed by the dreamer; individual insight alone is the key to understanding meaning. The following suggestions are offered only to help the beginner develop insight into symbolic thinking.

Most popular dream dictionaries border on fortune-telling and are not worth the paper they are printed on. However, two major books are considerable exceptions. If our abbreviated listing whets your curiosity, you might also gain additional insights from Cirlot's *Dictionary of Symbols,* a broad compilation of meanings, including exploration of archetypes.[1] The ultimate guide, Ad de Vries's *Dictionary of Symbols and Imagery,* can only be ordered directly from the publisher (Elsevier North-Holland, 52 Vanderbilt Avenue, New York, New York 10017).[2] The book is expensive and intended for the serious student. Definitions in these books particularly help one explore strange symbols and archetypes.

The following glossary reflects our discoveries of concepts, ideas, experiences, and images with relatively wide applications.

They are meant as nothing more than jump-starts to get you going on your tour of the Wilderness.

A

abandonment Generally, we are feeling unloved and unwanted. We may need to look carefully at current relationships and explore why they are failing. On the other hand, abandonment can signal leaving the past behind and finding freedom from old restraints.

abortion Men have abortions? Sure, if they are about to lose an important extension of themselves. We may be warned of impending disaster. Equally, we may be informed of the need to "jettison" something in which we have considerable emotional investment.

acne Any facial distortion may raise questions about concern for personal appearance. Are we afraid of leaving the wrong impression? By the same token, skin eruptions imply inner imbalance or infections. Have we failed to pay attention to an emotional issue that is ready to erupt?

actor Playing a role always raises questions about what is happening with our persona, the image we project. Are we living out a phony front? Is a deception being perpetrated? On the other hand, would we like to get out of the rut in which we're living? Maybe we've exhausted a social role and need to quit performing.

adultery The act itself breaks covenant with another by betrayal of trust. Are we selling someone out? Are we about to be sold out? While adultery can imply sexual infidelity, it is equally a powerful symbol of compromise and deception.

alcohol See *drunk*. The first question is, "How do you feel about alcohol consumption?" If you're a big drinker, is the dream a warning? On the other hand, a teetotaler might explore why the dream behavior is contrary to normal life. Drinking can be both a symbol of defiance as well as an indication of the need for relaxation. If an addiction is implied by the dream, we will want to consider whether an outside force has taken control of our lives. Don't forget Jesus turned water into wine. Wine also represents the blood of Christ. Wine can be a symbol of transformation.

altar   When we dream of candles, crosses, pulpits, and many other objects found in churches, we must first ask ourselves about the function of the particular entity. An altar is a place of sacrifice as well as personal commitment. We both meet God and take vows before an altar. Altars particularly signify the place where heaven and earth meet.

angels   The basic Greek word for angel simply means a messenger. A beginning point of inquiry is to ask if the symbol is bringing a special message.

ape   All animals potentially represent primitive drives and energies. The untamed, wild side of our nature is often represented by the beasts. We need to look at what a particular creature means to us. Why would we either admire or dislike the animal?

arms, weapons   Freud suggested we look in the direction of male sexuality. However, his view is too limited. Guns represent instruments of attack. If the assault is upon us, are we ignoring our conscience? On the other hand, assault on the Doorkeeper's control represents growth in the direction of greater personality integration.

art   Take a careful look at the pictures on the walls. What is depicted in the scenes? Chances are high you have inner needs and desires being illustrated. What do you see in the pictures that tells you about your emotional life?

attic See *house.* Every room in a house needs consideration for what it implies, i.e., kitchens are places of nurture; bedrooms are the settings for sexual activity. Since attics are places of storage, they often represent memories or references to the past.

B

baby Look carefully at the context. A baby can represent an extension of yourself. A project, a business, an idea, a creation can be symbolized by an infant. On the other hand, an infant could be part of some experience at the earliest stage of our lives.

band Are you "on parade"? Is the band suggesting you are a performer? Are you being swept along with the crowd? In contrast, a harmonious performance could suggest that the many parts of your personality are coming together in new concord.

baptism, bathing Always a powerful image, baptism can be a symbol of transformation. Inherent in the meaning is a change of heart and mind through cleansing. Baptism may represent a fresh start.

barroom Consider whether you frequent bars. Why or why not? English citizens see the pub as a place of friendly association. Many Americans see a bar as a clandestine place for questionable pursuits. Is the bar a scene from *Cheers* or is it a "Red Dog Saloon"? It is also possible a dream trip to a bar is compensatory for a need to escape from a lifestyle that is too rigid.

basement See *attic.* Is something "base" going on? Basements may be a place for hidden feelings or experiences.

bed See *attic.*

blacks The meaning of a black person in a dream depends on our racial background. Since aboriginal people are black, the color may indicate primitive characteristics or undeveloped portions of the personality. It can be the aspect of our personalities closest to nature. White people may dream of blacks as the "dark" side of the Shadow.

blindness Are we not paying attention? Remember, one function of dreams is to bring into consciousness facts we have ignored. Are we blind to an important truth?

blood Blood is the source of life, of vitality. While blood can represent close kinship, it can also signal "bad blood" between individuals. The loss of blood brings death.

bread Often called the "staff of life," bread can embody our physical needs or the need for sustenance. We receive energy from bread. In addition, bread is a symbol for the life of Christ.

breast In American society, the breast has become a primary symbol of sexuality. Therefore, a woman dreaming of revealing herself may signify a wish to exhibit either greater sensuality, femininity, or personal honesty. On the other hand, a dream of losing the breast can reveal a deep-seated fear of the loss of attractiveness or youthful beauty. While men may be drawn to the breast as a sexual stimulus, it is also the source of nurture and emotional well-being. The breast is the original place of feeding, of meeting primal needs.

broom Why are we sweeping? Are we trying to "clean house"? Does something need to be removed from our lives? Have we let old dirt pile up in our lives?

burglar Burglars are often symbols of being violated. They may be a warning that our conscious minds haven't noticed we are under attack by friends, family, or associates. We need to look carefully at what is being taken from us in the dream. At the same time, we may be the guilty party. Are we taking something that doesn't belong to us? Is our conscience accusing us with the image of a thief? In addition, women's dreams of forced entry can indicate a fear of sexual intercourse.

burns Look for a pun. Are we about to get "burned" in a relationship or a business deal? Are we involved in a situation that is actually "too hot to handle"?

butterfly A wonderful symbol of transformation. Like in the Resurrection, a form of life may be dying so that another more beautiful one may begin.

C

cancer An insidious disease that kills from within suggests we look for an inner source of emotional disease. Since cancer is an illness in which we literally destroy ourselves, consider whether it is a symbol of our being our own worst enemy.

candle Candles bring light into the darkness. They may suggest wisdom or the quest for understanding. We often think of candles as dispelling the darkness.

car Generally a symbol of the self. The condition and quality of the car will tell us a great deal about how we see ourselves. Is the car a sporty model or an old, dependable family style? How are the tires? Who is driving? Is the car out of control? Headed for a crash? What is happening with the car will tell us volumes about our current emotional and mental condition.

cards   Since card-playing is a game of chance more than skill, we will want to consider if the symbol is warning us about taking too large a risk. Is someone else "holding all the aces"? Life can be like a card game with unexpected gains and losses.

carnival   The medieval idea of a carnival was a time of pandering the flesh. Carnivals are frivolous occasions. The symbol can both suggest *I need to take a break* as well as *I'm about to make a fool of myself.*

castration   Classically the symbol represents the loss of male sexuality and loss of potency. One should look for the source of the castration. Who is holding the knife?

cat   See *ape.*

cemetery   While often assumed to be a sign of impending death, graves, tombs, and burial may more likely represent either a fear of death or be a symbol of transformation. We need to explore who has died and why. On the other hand, something may be buried in our memories or our pasts. In the same way, maybe we are about to be buried by present circumstances. Could someone be trying to bury you?

chain   Strong bonds can keep us in touch with important values or represent bondage. Are we being inhibited or supported by the dream chains?

child   An extremely important symbol, we must look carefully to see if the child is an extension of ourselves or a representation of our own childhood. We can be called to examine an early period in our lives. What is the condition of the child? Neglected? Happy? Do we need to pay attention to our inner child? A child is often a symbol of life. The Christ child, the divine child, represents God-given possibilities.

church See *altar.* Generally a symbol of our religious lives or our quest for God. The shape of the building or what happens inside may be a comment on the state of our spiritual lives or our religious journey. Consider what part of the church the dream is depicting. Just as parts of a house have significance, so can places in the church building give us specific direction about the dream message.

clock See *numbers.* Is the clock warning we are going too slow or too fast? Is time getting away from us, or could we be squandering our time? If the clock is about to strike midnight, you might guess you're close to the end of something important. Where are the hands on the clock? Often numbers represent our age when something important occurred.

clothes The way we are dressed in a dream can tell us volumes about how we currently see ourselves. Since dreams are compensatory, we may be confronted with a dimension of our personhood we are ignoring. For example, shoes often convey our general condition. Got a hole in the shoe? Run-down heels? Take a second look at how you feel about yourself. Low on sole (soul)? Running around in underwear or the lack of clothing can either indicate a desire for greater honesty or the fear of self-disclosure.

clown Do we need to stop being so rigid and start "clowning around" more? Then again, could we be making fools of ourselves and not realizing our overextension?

colors Colors signal a particularly important dream. In addition, we should note the hue of the color. Green can either be a vital color of growth or a sickly shade for illness. Fading colors may signal a loss of vitality in a particular virtue. The following denote mental attitudes.

232

Green: envy, nature, vitality, sickness

Red: passion, anger, personal warmth, love

Gold: wealth, regal value, the color for divinity

Blue: the sky, majesty covering, healing, or religious symbol

Brown: a symbol for depression, impending storm, dishonesty

Black: despair, loss of light

White: purity

compass   Could a compass be offering us correct direction? Warning that we are off course? The appearance of a compass might cause us to question our sense of direction.

coughing   Are we about to get sick? Check your temperature. In the opposite direction, could something be "stuck in our throats"? Do we need to get something off of our chests?

cross   Meanings of the cross are vast. Crosses are used both as gravemarkers and as a call to commitment. Bearing a cross can both be a symbol of a masochistic personal struggle and of a noble heroic effort. A cross can represent opposites coming together in perfect balance. If the dream seems to have religious content, we will want to consider the wide range of meanings of the cross within the Christian message. While the cross is a symbol of the suffering of Christ, it is also the ultimate sign of victory over death. A cross can be a sign of renewal and starting over again. We may be asked to bear a cross, or we may discover a current painful situation is valuable in God's sight as a place of redemption.

crossroads   Consider if you have come to an important place of decision. Are you overlooking how important the present moment in your life may be?

D

dance   Are you too uptight and need to "kick up your heels"? Maybe you need to become more spontaneous. At the same time you may be celebrating a great joy.

death   See Chapter 11.

debt   Have we buried something in our consciences? Maybe we are failing to meet an obligation we have to another person. Possibly we are living below someone's expectations.

deformity   Often deformed people emerge from the Shadow. They are generally unacceptable parts of ourselves. We haven't yet come to accept these dimensions of our personhood. A midget or dwarf often represents underdevelopment.

desert   Wandering across a desert is a sure sign of living in a dry, arid time in our lives. We may be feeling isolated or hopeless. On the other hand, we may be functioning without significant emotion. Maybe we should examine the "wellsprings" in our lives and see if anything has dried up.

devil   See "S-t-r-a-n-g-e Symbols," Chapter 12.

doctor   Doctors are both symbols of healing and wisdom. They may help us diagnose something that is sick. The figure may be offering healing or calling us to pay attention to a condition we have neglected.

dog   See *ape.*

door   Doors can represent both opportunity and repression. Is it time to enter a new period in our life? Are we failing to explore a previously closed portion of our experience?

drunk   We may be on the verge of going out of control. Some aspect of our lives may be out of control. On the other hand, could we be intoxicated with the ecstasy of a new relationship and not realize we are just a little drunk with infatuation?

E

egg   Eggs are often symbols of possibility. Potential and hope are natural messages from eggs. However, eggs are fragile and quite breakable. We could be warned not to put all of our eggs in one basket.

electricity   Empowerment and energy are suggested by electricity. Are the wires running into or out of us? Could you be running out of energy? Turned-off electricity can suggest depression. A live wire could be a warning of impending danger.

embalm   Consider carefully what or who is being embalmed. We may be trying to save something that is precious, or we may be perpetuating ideas and beliefs that need to be buried. The suggestion might be it's time to let go.

enema   Inner cleansing is expressed by this symbol. We may be emotionally or mentally constipated. Is the dream suggesting it's time to have a new openness toward ideas and beliefs we have ignored? By the same token, dreams of physical conditions always prompt us to take a second look at our bodies and any health irregularities.

epilepsy   Since this condition is a lack of physical control, we need to consider what may be out of control in our lives. Perhaps circumstances have gotten out of hand and we are being "jerked around." The problem may be we have lost control of our lives.

eye Consciousness and awareness are well symbolized by the eye. Are we blind? Are we seeing things others have missed? Could the eye be telling us to pay attention to what is being overlooked? For a different slant, reconsider the People Paradigm. The "I" in dreams can be an "eye." In these instances, we may be dealing with the Doorkeeper.

eyeglasses If you don't wear glasses, the dream could be suggesting you need to! On the other hand, maybe some important issues are out of focus. Are you not seeing things as clearly as you should? Could you possibly be looking out at the world through rose-colored glasses?

F

face Maybe something in your life needs to be "faced." Are you putting on a good face when you feel quite to the contrary? Could you be "two faced"? Faces can mask our inner feelings. The dream could be asking us to confront hidden issues.

factory We may feel our lives have become nothing more than an assembly-line bore! Everything may be a grind. Possibly, we've lost our individuality. Are we marching on a treadmill?

fall Is there a warning here? Could we be headed for a fall? For some people recurring dreams of falling may represent a strong fear of being out of control.

father Generally parents appear in dreams as themselves rather than as symbols. Often the issue is our relationship with this person. However, a father can represent God or an authority figure.

fear The most important issue in frightening dreams is to look at the solution phase of the dream. Since dreams bring good news, there is an answer in the final message about facing our fear.

fence We often dream of self-imposed or self-created barriers. What is the fence trying to keep out? Do we need to look over a barricade to see the other side?

fever We might be about to get sick. Fever could be a warning. On the other hand, we might experience psychological stress as a fever. Fevers are symptomatic of illness and could be calling us to look within the present social situation for pathology.

fire Recurring dreams of flames may suggest we need the help of a professional counselor to examine what's going on in our inner worlds. All persistent symbols of destruction are reasons for concern. On the other hand, fire is a symbol of purification. Error is possibly being purged.

fish Fish and creatures of the ocean float up from the unconscious mind. As lakes and seas are good symbols of the unconscious, so fish suggest inner material is "coming up." Going fishing might be a good way to express our desire to get in touch with the depths of our personality.

flowers Flowers are often given as gifts to convey affection. They are good symbols of positive emotion. However, dead flowers suggest affection has dried up.

flying Often a sign of exhilaration, we need to notice whether we are the pilot or are being "taken for a ride." Look for metaphors such as "flying high" or "heading for a crash." Are we missing what's going on in everyday life? Are we flying to or fleeing from?

Flying can be a good symbol to represent ambition. In addition, we may be ascending to great levels and heights of awareness giving us a very broad view of what is going on. In contrast, flying might suggest we are far too idealistic and not grounded sufficiently in our thinking.

fog What are you not seeing clearly? Why are you walking around in a daze?

friend When the friend is of the same sex, we can conjecture that the Shadow is offering a new relationship with an important aspect of ourselves. We will want to explore the characteristics of the friend.

frozen Often ice expresses shut-down emotions. We may need to explore why an emotional area of our lives is blocked.

G

garden As was true in the Garden of Eden, the garden is a place of fulfilled longings. Beautiful things grow in gardens. Therefore, this symbol may speak of developing possibilities. Do we need to cultivate the garden or enjoy it? Gardens can suggest areas for spiritual growth.

gasoline If the dream car is running out of gas, we are getting a signal about our energy levels.

geyser Eruptions should cause us to look for areas of suppressed pressure in our lives. Something may be ready to blow and we're not reading the signs.

giant Giants represent both big possibilities and problems too large to handle. Is the giant a friend or foe? Extremely tall people have the capacity for long-range perspective.

gold   Often a symbol of wealth, gold represents spiritual riches in many dreams. Because gold does not tarnish, it can describe eternal value.

guide   Wisdom figures appear to help us find new direction. They may bring gifts that increase our inner capacities. Needed new knowledge is often imparted through this person.

H

hair   Our "thought lives" are often reflected by hair. However, pubic hair has obvious sexual connotations, and a long white beard can refer to wisdom and authority. Loss of hair can suggest fear of diminishing strength or sexual capacity. Hair can express sensuality.

hammer   While a hammer is a natural symbol to express power, it can also refer to a penis. Hammering can convey indifferent use of too much force.

hell   When it's a symbol of the inner world, hell can tell us just how bad things are inside us. We may be getting in touch with our depth of pain over certain issues. On the other hand, we may be receiving a warning about the destiny our present behavior is leading toward.

hill   A mountain can present us with a great challenge worthy of our best energy. We may be called to reach a new height beyond any previous attainment.

horse   See *ape*. Horses fascinate us because of the sleek instinctive energy they represent. Sexual connotations are associated with stallions. Wild horses symbolize both freedom and unrestrained independence. Often they suggest a repressed drive ready to break loose.

hospital See *doctor.* Hospitals are places for recovering and help when we are sick. Because operations happen there, we may need to explore whether an attitude or problem needs to be removed from our lives. A hospital in the dreamscape is a good indication of a need for healing.

house See *attic* and *basement.* The house is usually a symbol of the self, and few symbols are as universal and occur as often as a representation of the dreamer. Every part of a house has meaning. For example, the kitchen is a place of nurture where we are sustained and difficult things become palatable. We need to look carefully at the condition of the house. What are the style and period it represents? What shape is the foundation in? Is the roof attached securely?

hunger Something in our lives is not being nourished. We are neglecting a vital area that needs our attention.

husband See *wife.*

I

idiot One aspect of ourselves is totally unacceptable and living in exile in the Wilderness. Often this Shadow dimension appears as the idiot needing to be loved and nurtured.

impotence Fear of being weak or losing strength may appear in this symbolic form. On the other hand, sexual incapacity and inability can surface in this mode.

indigestion Maybe it would have been better not to have eaten that pizza before going to bed! However, you may be in a personal situation you can't "stomach" right now.

infection Could someone be spreading "germs" in your values and ideals? Is the unconscious asking you to recognize an insidious invasion that could "sap" you?

island Often we are feeling isolated, cut off from the main source of things. Possibly our emotions are not hooked up to our thoughts. We may want to explore if we are feeling lonely these days.

J

jail Are we locked in? Has our present situation become too confining? On the other hand, maybe our conscience is suggesting a penalty needs to be paid for our recent transgressions.

jam Rather than marmalade for breakfast, we may be revisiting a sticky mess we're in.

jewels First, explore what jewelry means to you. How does receiving or possessing expensive gems make you feel? This perspective gives a setting for the meaning of a particular gem.
Pearls: turning adversity and suffering into beauty
Ruby: a symbol of love
Diamonds: the eternal symbol of ultimate value
Emeralds: symbols of growth

joker See *clown*. Batman movies have developed a new meaning of a crazy dangerous figure who uses humor for destruction.

jury A strong symbol of the conscience. We need to examine the issues being presented to the jury.

K

key Freud would suggest sexual activity. We might look at opening hidden areas, unleashing new potential, and setting repressed dimensions of the personality free.

king This symbol could be a way of referring to our fathers. What does the king do to us, and how does he make us feel? Is he a good or a bad king?

knife Often suggests the male sex organ.

knight Girls are often looking for a "knight in shining armor" to rescue them. Boys identify with knights in their quest to prove manhood. The knight is also a strong archetype of the quest for holy meaning and purpose.

L

ladder Jacob's great dream used the ladder as a symbol of reaching God. Ladders offer us a series of steps to reach the top. Therefore, the ladder may be a symbol of encouragement to reach higher attainment than we thought possible.

lamb Christians generally associate the lamb with Jesus, the Good Shepherd. Lambs are both symbols of innocence and incompetence. They also represent gentleness.

lantern See *candle.*

laundry We've got dirty laundry needing our attention!

leaper See *idiot.* In addition, the symbol can suggest the loss of social respectability.

lemon Sourness could suggest we are leaving a bad taste in someone's mouth. Defective cars can also be lemons! On another level, the lemon can imply bitterness.

library Accumulated wisdom available to us is suggested by a library. We may be pointed to a source of wisdom we didn't know existed.

M

madness   See *idiot*. May represent the fear of loss of rational control and being overwhelmed by forces beyond our control. The symbol might suggest we are close to the edge.

mail   Letters are a way the unconscious can send us a message. Mail can be a special device to get our attention.

maps   Much like mail, a map can give us a special message or a picture of what lies ahead and the direction we should take. Often studying the dream map can impart crucial new insights.

marriage   See *wedding*.

Mary   The Virgin Mary can represent the soul of humanity. Orthodox Christianity calls her the *Theotokos,* the God-bearer who brings the Christ. She is the ultimate symbol of the lowly and poor being exalted by God. Since Mary's role is to point to her Son, we may explore how she leads us toward redemption.

mermaid   As creatures of the ocean, mermaids represent figures arising out of the unconscious. Often they represent love or a call from the deepest part of us to love.

mirror   Remembering the principle that we can't see the back of our head, dreams show us what we otherwise aren't able to see. Dream mirrors usually have such a function. What is hidden often can be seen in the mirror, creating a deeper awareness of the self.

monks   Priests, ministers, nuns, and monks are strong symbols of religious teaching and insight. They may appear to impart spiritual wisdom and understanding. Monastic figures may also embody a desire to retreat from the world.

monster Everyone has the capacity to do monstrous things. We must be realistic about what unrestrained emotion can cause. The monster may confront us with innate destructive capacities. On the other hand, the monster could embody powerful negative emotions surging upward trying to overpower us. Hate, fear, or anger might be on the rampage in the Wilderness. The specter needs to be examined carefully to understand the scope of the threat.

moon Think of "harvest moon" or "honeymoon"—romance is in the air. On the other hand, the word *lunatic* comes from *lunar.* Lunacy was thought to come from the attraction of the moon. Therefore, the moon can also be a symbol of irrational impulsive feelings.

mother See *father.*

mummy See *embalm.* Are we trying to preserve something that needs to be buried?

music Music is a source of peace and well-being. The symbol may suggest inner harmony and could signal things are going well.

N

nakedness Could we be afraid of being exposed? Maybe we don't feel secure with who we really are. On the other hand, we may wish for greater emotional disclosure.

name While we consider names only to be social designations, biblical names convey meaning that describes the essence of the person. Names can tell us who we really are. Explore a dream name to find the emotion and significance it embodies. Symbolically names can reveal how we really see ourselves.

newspaper   See *mail.*

numbers   One of the first things to consider is whether a number suggests our age when an important event occurred in our lives. The hands of a clock may be pointing to our age. In addition, numerology describes how numbers express ideas as much as convey quantities; biblical numbers are often of this order. Therefore, we can also ponder the meaning of numbers.

Zero can express nothingness and meaninglessness. Since *one* is indivisible, it often suggests a beginning point. *Two* can be divided into halves and may be suggesting the combination of opposites. *Three* represents a triangle. Because *four* can signify four corners, the number is a good representation of stability. The world was created and God rested in *seven* days, a good number for completion. *Ten* suggests a complete system. *Twelve* is a strong biblical number recalling the twelve tribes and the twelve apostles; twelve implies a complete unit. More complex numbers can suggest an arrangement and combination of these ideas.

nun   See *monks.*

nurse   Nurses are symbols of care and consolation. They may appear in dreams to offer us nurture and healing. Nurses can represent our need for mothering and warmth.

O

obscene   Repression doesn't make things go away! Like an iceberg, suppressed urges and needs come up somewhere else. Obscene events may be trying to get us to face ignored impulses or experiences. Rather than running, we need to take a hard look at the unseen and find out what the problem is.

ocean   See *water.*

odors   Perfume manufacturers know smells evoke emotion. A scent can either signal attraction or repulsion. A bad smell can tell us something rotten is going on.

officer   See *king.* Is the person a police officer or a military figure? Police figures can be sent from the conscience. Sergeants and generals could be trying to whip some order into our lives.

oil   We oil squeeky wheels. Oil can be turned into gasoline. Oil is also healing. Olive oil was a biblical symbol of healing and peace. Look for a possible metaphor such as "pouring oil on troubled waters." On the other hand, if the dream figure is an "oily person," there's a warning in the dream for us.

operation   See *doctor* and *hospital.*

orchestra   See *band.*

orphan   See *abandonment.* We feel lost and parentless. Possibly we are feeling deeply misunderstoo

ostrich   An ostrich may be a rather strong suggestion we may have "our heads in the sand."

oven   The oven is a good symbol of transformation. The heat in an oven changes dough into bread. During a hot and difficult time, an oven might reassure us something good is going to come out of our trials.

owl   See *ape*. Owls are particularly symbols of wisdom. The Plains Indians believed owls to have great power; owls were often seen as symbols of death. Since owls see well at night, they suggest wisdom that penetrates darkness.

ox   See *ape*.

oyster   Take another look at *oven*. Oyster could be a similar symbol of transformation if there is a pearl inside the oyster. We may want to use active imagination and pry the dream oyster apart. Current problems may be filled with possibility.

P

parachute   Are we heading for a nasty fall and the dream is offering us an escape? Look at the symbol as a means of either overcoming or avoiding our fear of a fall.

paralysis   A common dream experience is trying to run as fast as possible but not being able to move. The problem is inadequacy. Could we be afraid of an approaching test of our abilities? A problem we don't know how to solve? The dream may put us in touch with our deep-seated guilt or apprehension.

parasite   Is the parasite a person or a condition? Is a horrible-looking creature crawling around in the dream? Dream creatures can sneak inside and sap our strength. We may be overlooking how seriously we are being undermined.

parents   See *father*.

pariah   See *idiot*.

party   Often a party suggests a need to lighten up. Maybe we are simply working too hard. On the other hand, the dreamscape may be telling us we aren't taking current responsibilities seriously enough.

pawnshop Have we put life on hold? Have we given up control of something that is very dear to us? Is it time to take back an aspect of our lives we've put on the shelf?

perfume See *odors.*

perspiration Sweating suggests intense expenditure of energy or effort. We may be underestimating the pressure we are under.

photographs, pictures See *art.* Pictures evoke memories. We will want to look carefully at any representation of ourselves and note how the dream picture is different from our current countenance. Are we younger? Are we aging? Hard or embittered? Distorted?

pig See *ape.* Pigs are symbols of dirtiness and slovenly habits. Are we about to "wallow in the mud"? Is greed turning us into real "swine"? Is a dream figure wearing a pig's head? Could this be a warning of "pig-headedness"?

pilgrim See *knight.* These figures represent a journey toward lofty dreams and holy adventures. This could be a good representation of the self's drive for realization.

pit Ever feel like your life is the "pits"? We may fear the same condition in our lives will bury us or that we can't escape threatening circumstances. Pay careful attention to the solution phase of the dream.

plumbing See *house.* Broken plumbing can be a strong warning about something breaking loose in our lives. An emotion may be exploding. Watch out. You could "drown" or have your "house" ruined by such a ruptured pipe.

pocket See *clothes*. Because we keep things there, pockets are good symbols for memory. What do you find in your dream pockets?

potter, pottery The potter's craft depends on the wad of clay being centered on the wheel. We may be challenged to see if our lives are on center.

pregnancy A great symbol for promise or new possibility. Possibly we are ready to give birth to a new idea, a new project, or a new dream. Maybe a new reality is ready to be birthed.

priest See *monks*.

prison See *pit*. We create our own prisons from the fears, inhibitions, attitudes, and limitations of childhood. Prisons reflect severe inadequacies.

prostitution Are we selling ourselves for financial gain? Are we compromising the best we have to offer?

puppet Could we be manipulated by present circumstances? By people? Or might the dream be telling us we are the manipulators?

Q

queen See *father*. This symbol could represent our mothers. Women may also want to see themselves in a regal role.

quicksand We need to beware! We're getting swallowed by something from which we cannot escape. We could be "getting in over our heads" without realizing how serious a current situation is.

quiz Often people dream of not being able to pass an exam. Such dreams reflect a sense of inadequacy. We may be afraid of dealing with an immediate problem.

R

rabbi See *monks*.

rabbit See *ape*. Rabbits can have a sexual connotation. Is the dream rabbit a *Playboy* bunny? Get the picture?

radio See *art, library, mail*.

railway Railway stations and terminals often represent crossroads or places to change direction. A train can be a strong suggestion of a journey we are on. We need to examine carefully if the dream is telling us to change trains now or a warning we are about to miss the train.

rainbow A wonderful symbol of harmony and peace, a rainbow may tell us we have achieved an important goal. We are at a place of inner peace.

rape The ultimate crime of violation and abuse suggests we are being desecrated, defiled, and forced into an outrageous bind. We must take very seriously where the source of the problem is. Women must explore the physical implications of such dreams.

rats Mice, rodents, and rats are often a warning. We may be involved with someone who is a real "rat." Does the dream suggest you need to "smell a rat" in the situation at hand?

refrigerator   See *frozen*.

restaurant   Explore what eating out means to you. Is it a matter of convenience? Privilege? Does being waited on make you feel special? Then explore what sort of place the dream café is. Elegant? Fast food? Sloppy Joe's? Restaurants can also represent sociability.

river   See *water*. Can be a good symbol to express our flow of energy, life force. Rivers of living water are a biblical expression for vitality imparted by the Holy Spirit. Baptism can happen in a stream suggesting cleansing.

road   See *railway*. Roads are strong suggestions of our life journey or destiny.

rock   The psalmist often speaks of God as being a rock and a fortress. Rocks are symbols of stability and eternal strength. They offer reassurance of permanency. In the Old Testament, rocks commemorate special achievements and encounters with God. The dream rock may be a sign of encouragement. Watch out that the rock isn't suggesting you've become hard-headed.

running   People often wake up from a night of continual running and getting nowhere. The race could tell us we aren't facing an issue that won't go away. The problem could be an emotion we must face. On the other hand, maybe we aren't really going anywhere! The dream could be a suggestion of how futile our lives have become. Are we running on a treadmill?

S

sabotage   Because dreams inform and create awareness, sabotage may suggest we are ignoring a threat to our well-being.

sailors   See *ship*. What is the sailor doing? May tell us how we are handling some aspect of our voyage through life.

saint   See *monks*.

Satan   See Chapter 12.

scales   The balance scales of justice represent the quest for equity. We may be concerned we are being treated unfairly, or the dream could be asking us to consider if we are perpetrating injustice in our own dealings with people.

scars   We need to explore past memories. Possibly we have ignored just how serious a past experience was.

school   Like a house or church, school is a strong symbol of personal involvement. Schools are places of instruction. From grade school to college, we will want to explore what happened during our education. We need to discover what the educational institution meant to us.

scissors   Jabbing motions with scissors can suggest sexual intercourse. In contrast, scissors also express aggression through cutting remarks or jabbing insults.

scroll   See *art, library, mail*.

searchlight   Look at what the light is revealing. Our attention is called to a particular issue.

sex   See Chapter 11.

shampoo   Symbols of cleansing suggest a quest for freedom from guilt. On the other hand, washing something out of our hair is a good way of getting free of an involvement.

sharks See *ape*. Loan sharks prey on unsuspecting needy victims. The symbol might be telling us we are about to get "bitten."

ship See *car*. A boat is often a symbol of the self and our journey through the world. Stormy seas can tell us how we are feeling about current struggles.

sleep Dreaming of being asleep reflects a lack of awareness. The dream may be telling us to wake up. On the other hand, sleeping may suggest we are trying to escape reality.

snake Snakes are more complicated symbols than one might expect. Generally thought of as sinister images of temptation, snakes are also used as a sign of health and eternal life. Because snakes shed their skin, they imply rebirth. The ancient physician's staff had intertwined snakes. In some cultures snakes are symbols of wisdom. On the other hand, we refer to unscrupulous people as "snakes in the grass."

snow See *frozen*.

spear Think through how the spear is used. Are people jabbed? Could the thrusts be aggressive attacks? Does the spear represent anger? Take a look at what you say to people. Words can be more deadly than arrows.

spider Spiders spin webs. Are we currently caught in a seductive situation? The dream might be telling us to beware. For many people, the spider is a symbol of their mother's unhealthy control and manipulation of their lives.

staircase   See *ladder.* Steps can suggest an orderly process toward a goal or objective. Often climbing up the stairs reflects movement toward sexual fulfillment and climax. In contrast, ladders can suggest striving toward the top of the social or business world.

steam   See *geyser.*

storm   Emotional turmoil creates storms. The turbulence may be recreating what's happening in our inner worlds so we can get the problem out on the table.

submarine   See *fish.* Subs are excellent symbols of our journey through the unconscious. Subs signal we are in touch with the depths of our personalities.

swans   These beautiful birds are wonderful symbols of transformation. Just as ugly ducklings turn into creatures of beauty, so the self emerges with glory.

swimming   Swimming suggests skimming across the top of the unconscious and moving through our feelings. Consider your swimming style. An inability to swim suggests we aren't handling emotions well, but confident swimming tells us the opposite message. If we are threatened by the water we can guess we have serious reservations about facing feelings.

sword   Swords can have majestic meaning. See *knight.* A sword could be a symbol of the quest for truth. Scripture is called the sword of the Spirit. Perhaps we are using a blade to protect others. On the other hand, we will want to check and make sure we are not hurting anyone. What we thought was righteous action could be the cause of malicious damage.

T

table We get things "out on the table" when we need to deal with them. Have we seen the table before? If so, it may give us a context for what we should be considering.

tail In slang, *tail* suggests a sexual connotation. Because it is an extension of the spine, a tail can suggest we have a great deal of backbone or strength.

tailor Because tailors fix our clothes, they suggest we may need to work on our ideas or values. The appearance of a tailor may tell us we have some alteration work to do on our opinions or thoughts.

tangle We may be more confused and in a bigger muddle than we recognize. Are we hopelessly mixed up?

target Targets are good representations of our goals and objectives. Are we hitting the bull's-eye? Missing the mark?

tattoo See *scars*. Has something "gotten under our skin" that simply won't go away? Look at the tattoo and see if it tells you what must be faced.

tavern See *barroom*.

teeth Do we have a comment here on our physical appearance? Could we be "losing face"? We also may be guilty of making biting remarks. It might not hurt to have a dental checkup.

telegram See *mail, telephone*.

telephone People may wake up to a telephone ringing and discover their bedside phone hasn't rung. Such experiences call us to wake up to something significant happening around us. Since phones are means of communication, they are symbols of "getting in touch."

television See *mail, telephone.*

thorn Something stuck us, and it still hurts. Look for an unresolved source of pain.

thread What's held together with a thread? Watch out! The situation is about to break apart.

tire See *car.* Any part of a car causes us to consider the meaning of the automobile. Tires keep cars on the road. Are we running out of air? Got a flat? We will want to ponder what is slowing our lives down.

tramp See *idiot.* This could be a desire to escape and "tramp around" the country. Don't forget Charlie Chaplin's little tramp character. The innocent little man was the ultimate survivor.

trapeze See *flying.* Could we be taking unnecessary risks?

tree Trees are powerful symbols of strength and endurance. The tree of life offers great spiritual encouragement. The cross of Christ can be represented by the tree. Our lives could be represented by a tree with a root system representing where we begin as we grow up toward the sky.

truck See *car, van.*

tunnels Long, dark passageways suggest we are entering a mysterious stage of our journey toward wholeness. The symbol may represent our uncertainty about what comes next.

turtle   Could the hard shell suggest we're "thick-skinned" or emotionally impenetrable? Are we likely to retreat instead of push forward? On the other hand, the turtle reassures us that slow, steady progress will win the race.

typewriter   The issue may well be what is coming out of the typewriter. What is the message? See *mail, telephone.*

U

umbrella   Is the dream warning us to come prepared for unexpected storms? Chances are the storm is emotional in nature.

undressing   See *nakedness.* Such a dream could warn us of confiding too much in someone we trust.

uniform   Are we wearing the uniform? Why? We may be trying to conform to some idea, group, or image. The need to wear a uniform may indicate a lack of self-confidence in our identities.

university   Did you attend college? If so you might want to explore what this period in your life meant. If not, you might ponder how you feel about the idea of attending a university. Are you turned off by intellectuals? Do you feel a need for further personal development? Universities are places of personal development.

urine   Maybe we just need to get up and go to the bathroom. However, the symbol can also suggest a need to release tensions. In modern slang it can suggest anger.

usher   This could be a wisdom figure trying to guide us to our proper place. Let the usher take you where he or she will.

V

vacation   Dreaming of life in Hawaii? Maybe you need to face up to living on a treadmill. Possibly you ought to take a vacation. On the other hand, could the dream be telling you someone else is on a vacation when he or she ought to be working for you?

valley   Going down into valleys can suggest a difficult time in our lives. "Down in the valley" might point toward depression. It could also suggest female sex organs.

vampire   This symbol of living death that preys on people would be a strong suggestion that someone or something is sucking the life out of us.

van   See *car.* Could we be hauling lots of baggage around in our lives? Maybe the van suggests we need to move on to another place in our life journey.

ventriloquist   Take a look at who is the dummy. Is someone turning us into his or her mouthpiece? On the other hand, could we be manipulating our children, our spouse, or our friends?

virgin   Virginity suggests a time of innocence and purity. It could represent a time in our lives when we were uncorrupted. In this sense, virginity might signal uncorrupted personal standards. See *Mary.*

volcano   See *geyser.*

vulture   See *vampire.* Could someone be preying on our weaknesses? Or could we be the vultures? Take a look at what you are doing to persons of lesser capacity.

W

wade See *swimming, water.*

walking Walks around the dreamscape often suggest our present situations in life. We should consider where we seem to be headed in our walks. Are we getting nowhere? Going backward? Enjoying the stroll?

wall See *fence.*

wallet Our means of identification are carried in a wallet, or billfold. Thus wallets can tell us volumes about who we are. Could the dream purse be offering information on our identities? On the other hand, our security is tied to the place we keep our money. If we've lost the dream wallet, the dream may be warning us about how secure (or insecure) things are with us.

war Are our conflicts escalating into something more serious than we might imagine? Maybe we are being pushed toward violent response. On the other hand, are we at war with ourselves? Are the inner conflicts about to tear us apart?

water See *fish, swimming.* A strong suggestion of the unconscious, the soul, the self. Often oceans can represent the vastness of the unconscious mind. Great amounts of inner material are hidden beneath the surface. Lakes, ponds, and reservoirs can signal we are looking into the hidden portions of our minds and emotions. We need to look at the color of the water. Is it muddy and murky? Clear? The color can tell us about the state of things.

weakness   In the dream we may feel overwhelmed by a situation and lack the strength to resist. No matter what is done, we don't seem to have the capacity to stand up to the problem. The problem may be a symbol of our lack of inner resolve. Are we afraid to say no to a current problem or confrontation? Possibly we are not facing a significant flaw in our personalities. The dream may tell us it's time to deal with a character defect.

wealth   Are we worried about financial security? Possibly we are too preoccupied with accumulation. On the other hand, the symbol might be leading us toward our true wealth we've over-looked.

weather   See *storm*. Weather is used to express many metaphors. Clouds with silver linings indicate a happy ending is ahead. We say people have a "stormy" personality, a gloomy disposition. Look for weather to be a symbol of mood or conditions surrounding your life. Clouds can suggest depression or an impending difficulty. The complete range of emotion can be expressed through weather conditions. Look at the weather report the dream offers as a commentary on what's ahead in your emotional world.

wedding   Weddings are good symbols for transformation. They suggest inner unification of diverse parts of our personalities. See Chapter 11 and the discussion of sexual dreams. On the other hand, we may be looking at a representation of how we feel about our own or potential marriage.

weeds   Got weeds in the garden? Take a look at your ideas, thoughts, and values. Remember the parable of the wheat and the tares in the Bible. Maybe you need to pull something out!

werewolf   See *vampire*. Archetypal horror stories probably begin as an expression of the human potential to be so completely consumed by animal impulses that rationality is destroyed and murderous impulses are unleashed. Is the dream warning that we are close to being out of control? Is someone else dangerous?

widow Don't panic and worry you're about to lose your spouse. You may simply need some significant time alone.

wife Our spouse can be a strong symbol of the Alter-Gender and may represent this dimension of our personalities. Therefore, what the spouse does in the dream may reflect what we are doing in real life. Look at the figure as possibly depicting projection. On the other hand, we may want to look carefully to see if the dream is telling us something about the current state of affairs in our relationship with our spouse. Are there any indications here of how things are going in the marriage?

wig See *hair*. Could the symbol be suggesting artificiality? Since hair often represents our thought life, a wig could point to deception.

window See *house*. Our "outlook" on life is often suggested by the window.

wine Often a symbol of joy, wine can represent happiness and health. Jesus turned water into wine. In dreams, wine sometimes represents the presence of Christ in holy Communion. If alcohol consumption is a problem, look for the opposite connotations.

witch Mother can appear as a witch, an image suggesting we are either victimized by our emotions about her or maybe haven't faced how we really feel. Maybe we are treating other people in a "witchy" manner.

wolf See *ape, werewolf.*

wreck Does your dream put you in a car wreck? Watch out! You may be living too fast and reckless. Car wrecks are important warnings to look at emotional health. You may be far too overextended.

X Y Z

X rays Could we be so transparent someone is seeing through us? Are you possibly feeling exposed?

yardstick Measuring devices suggest we should examine issues and ideas. Are we "coming up short"? Maybe we need to be more exact.

yoke Could we be feeling unequally yoked with someone? A spouse? A business associate? Then again we may feel like a beast of burden. What are we dragging behind us?

zero See *numbers.*

zircon Artificial reproductions of diamonds might suggest we are settling for a cheap substitute for the real thing.

zoo See *ape.* Possibly our instinctive urges are caged up and need to be released. On the other hand, the dream could be offering us reassurance we have this side of our lives under control.

APPENDIX

Biblical References to Dreams

This is a listing of all biblical references to dreams, visions, looking, eyes, and seers.

Genesis
3:5–7
15:1
18:2
20:3, 6
21:19
28:12
31:10–12, 24
37:5–6, 810, 19–20
40:5–9, 16
41:1, 5, 7–8, 25–26, 32
42:9
46:2, 4

Exodus
3:1–6
16:9–11
24:15–18
25:1

Numbers
12:6
21:8
22:31

24:2–4, 15–16

Deuteronomy
6:8
11:18
13:1–5
29:2–4

Joshua
5:13–15

Judges
6:12–14
7:13–17

1 Samuel
3:3–10, 15
9:9–11, 15–19
28:6, 15

2 Samuel
7:4–10, 17
15:27
24:11
24:12

1 Kings
3:5–15
6:15–17

2 Kings
17:13

1 Chronicles
9:22
17:15
21:10, 16
25:5–7
26:28–29

2 Chronicles
9:29
12:15
16:7–10
19:2
26:5
29:25–26, 30
32:32
33:18–19
35:15

Job
4:14–16
7:13–14
20:8
33:15–16

Psalms
5:3
13:3
25:15
89:19

119:18
123:1–2
141:8

Proverbs
29:18

Ecclesiastes
5:3, 7

Isaiah
1:1
6:1–10
8:17
17:7–8
21:2
22:1, 5
28:7
29:8, 10–11
30:10
33:17
40:26
42:18–20
44:18

Jeremiah
5:21
8:15
14:4
23:16, 25, 27–28, 32
29:8, 21

Lamentations
2:9

Ezekiel
1:1, 4
2:9
7:13, 26
8:3–5, 7
10:1, 9
11:1, 24
12:2, 22–27
13:7, 16
40:2, 4, 6
43:1–6
44:1, 4, 5
46:19
47:2

Daniel
1:17
2:1–9, 19, 26, 28, 36
4:5–10, 13, 18–19
7:1–2, 7, 13, 15
8:1–3, 13, 15–18, 26-27
9:21–24
10:1, 5–16
11:14
12:5   .

Hosea
12:10

Joel
2:28

Amos
7:12

Obadiah
1:1

Micah
3:6–7

Nahum
2:2

Habakkuk
2:2–3

Zechariah
1:18
2:1
4:2
5:1, 5, 9
6:1
10:2
13:4

Matthew
1:20
2:12–13, 19, 22
13:15–16
17:9
27:19

Mark
8:18
9:8

Luke
1:22
24:23, 31

John
12:40
Acts
1:10
2:17
7:55
9:10–12
10:3–4
11:17
16:10
18:9
26:18–9
28:27

Romans
11:8, 10

2 Corinthians
4:18
12:1
Ephesians
1:18

Hebrews
11:10

Revelation
1:10, 14
4:1–3
5:6
6:8
9:17
14:1, 14
15:5

NOTES

Chapter 1
Dream Trails

1. Psalm 66:11–12.
2. Psalm 91:1, 3.
3. Psalm 90:12.

Chapter 2
Opening the Secrets of the Night

1. Matthew 7:3–5. See also Luke 6:41–42.
2. Ann Faraday, *The Dream Game* (New York: HarperCollins, 1990).
3. Ullman Monague and Nan Zimmerman, *Working with Dreams* (New York: Dell, 1979), 83.
4. Lawrence Kubie, "Blocks to Creativity," *International Science and Technology*.

Chapter 3
Getting in Touch

1. Robert Frost, "The Road Not Taken," originally published in *Mountain Interval* (New York: Henry Holt and Co., 1916).
2. Clark E. Moustakas, *Creativity and Conformity* (New York: Van Nostrand Reinhold, 1967).

Chapter 4
Tuning In

1. Frances G. Wickes, *The Inner World of Choice* (New York: Harper and Row, 1963).

Chapter 5
The Windmills of Your Mind

1. P. D. Ouspensky, *In Search of the Miraculous* (London: Routledge & Kegan Paul, 1950).
2. Joel 2:25.
3. Jonathan Winson, Ph.D., "The Meaning of Dreams," *Scientific American,* November 1990, 86–96.

Chapter 6
The Tunnel to Your Soul

1. See Daniel 7.
2. See Daniel 4.
3. See Genesis 41.
4. See Genesis 28:12-13, 19.

Chapter 7
Discernment

1. Jeremiah 17:9.
2. Philip Schaff, ed., *Nicene and Post-Nicene Fathers,* vol. VI (Grand Rapids: Eerdmans, 1991).
3. Carl Jung, "Psychology and Alchemy," in *The Collected Works of C. G. Jung,* vol. 12 (New York: Bollingen Foundation, 1944), Par. 12.

Chapter 8
Reading the Handwriting on the Wall

1. The quest for understanding is a normal insight producing function of the imagination. Any novelist can describe similar experiences when characters in his or her book seemed to come to life, find their own voices, and start telling their stories. Teachers often find their best insights appear spontaneously while teaching. New and unexplored ideas "pop out" while making a point. Active imagination is a profoundly creative tool for new discoveries.

Chapter 9
The Language of the Spirit

1. Douglas Groothuis, *Unmasking the New Age* (Downers Grove, Ill: InterVarsity, 1986); *Confronting the New Age: How to Resist a Growing Religious Movement* (InterVarsity, 1988); *Revealing the New Age Jesus: Challenges to Orthodox Views of Christ* (InterVarsity, 1990).

2. Thomas Molnar, *The Pagan Temptation* (Grand Rapids: Eerdmans, 1987).

3. Robert Morey, "When Christians Meet Astrology," *The Christian Herald,* December 1988, 23.

4. See Genesis 15:17–21.

5. See Genesis 28:12–13 RSV.

6. See Genesis 41.

7. See Genesis 40:5.

8. See Numbers 12:6–8 RSV.

9. See 1 Samuel 3, 28:6.

10. See Matthew 1 and 2

11. Acts 2:17

12. See Acts 10

13. See Acts 16:9-10.

14. See Isaiah 29:7 and Daniel 2:19.

15. See Genesis 22:11; Exodus 3:2; Numbers 22:22; and Judges 6:11.

16. See Matthew 27:19.

17. See Revelation 9:17.

18. See Luke 1:22.

19. See Acts 2:17.

20. See Leviticus 19:26 and Deuteronomy 18:10.

21. Louis M. Savory, Patricia H. Berne, and Strephon Kaplan Williams, Dreams and Spiritual Growth, A Christian Approach to Dream Work (New York: Paulist Press, 1984), 51.

22. Ibid., 53

Chapter 10
Hearing God

1. Saint Jerome, *Letter XXII, to Eustochium,* 30.

2. 2 Corinthians 12:9.

3. *The Life of the Rev. John Newton* (Oradell, N.J.: American Tract Society, 28ff.

4. Savory, Berne, Williams, *Dreams and Spiritual Growth,* 210.

5. Aniela Jaffé, *C. G. Jung, Word and Image,* Bollingen Series 97:2 (Princeton, N.J.: Princeton University Press, 1979).

Chapter 11
Transformation

1. Calvin Hill, *The Meaning of Dreams* (New York: McGraw-Hill, 1966), 36.

2. De Ropp, *The Master Game* (New York: Delacorte/Seymour Lawrence, 1968), 93.

Chapter 12
Pump Primers

1. Paul Meier, *The Third Millennium* (Nashville, Tenn.: Thomas Nelson, 1993).
2. Savory, Berne, and Williams, *Dreams and Spiritual Growth*, 212.
3. Herman Riffel, *Your Dreams: God's Neglected Gift* (Lincoln, Va.: Chosen Books, 1981), 117.

Chapter 13
Encouragement

1. C. G. Jung, "Psychology and Alchemy," *The Collected Works of C. G. Jung,* vol. 12, paragraph 12.

More Pump Primers

1. J. E. Cirlot, *Dictionary of Symbols* (New York: Philosophical Library, 1962).
2. Ad de Vries, *Dictionary of Symbols and Imagery* (New York: Elsevier, 1976).

BIBLIOGRAPHY

Books

The Ante-Nicene Fathers. Grand Rapids, Mich.: Eerdmans, various dates.

Aquinas, Saint Thomas. *The Summa Theologica,* trans. the Fathers of the English Dominican Province. New York: Benziger Bros.

Arndt, W. F., and F. W. Gingrich. *A Greek-English Lexicon of the New Testament.* Chicago: University of Chicago Press, 1952.

Artemidorus (Artemidorus Daldianus). Translated by Robert Wood. *The Interpretation of Dreams,* 10th ed. London: Robert Wood, 1690.

Babylonian Talmud, 2nd ed. Translated by Michael L. Rodkinson. New York: New Talmud, 1901.

Bergson, Henri. *The World of Dreams.* New York: Philosophical Library, 1958.

Brown, Francis, S. R. Driver, and Charles A. Briggs. *A Hebrew and English Lexicon of the Old Testament.* Oxford: Clarendon Press, 1907.

Bruer, Joseph, and Sigmund Freud. *Studies in Hysteria.* Boston: Beacon Press, 1961.

Cayce, Hugh Lynn, Tom C. Clark, and Shane Miller. *Dreams: The Language of the Unconscious.* Virginia Beach, Va.: A.R.E. Press, 1966.

Cirlot, J. E. *Dictionary of Symbols.* New York: Philosophical Library, 1962.

Cruden, Alexander. *Cruden's Complete Concordance to the Old and New Testaments.* New York: Holt, Rinehart & Winston, 1949.

De Ropp, Robert S. *The Master Game.* New York: Delacorte/Seymour Lawrence, 1968.

de Vries, Ad. *Dictionary of Symbols and Imagery.* Amsterdam: North Holland Publishing, 1974.

Duchesne, Monsignor Louis. *Early History of the Christian Church,* Vols. 2-3. London: John Murry, 1938.

Eliade, Mircea. *Myths, Dreams and Mysteries.* New York: Harper & Brothers, 1960.

Ellis, Havelock. *The World of Dreams.* London: Constable and Company, 1915.

Fedotov, G. P. *A Treasury of Russian Spirituality.* New York: Sheed & Ward, 1948.

Forham, Freida. *An Introduction to Jung's Psychology.* New York: Penguin, 1953.

Freud, Sigmund. *Collected Papers of Sigmund Freud.* New York: Basic Books, 1959.

———. *A General Introduction to Psychoanalysis.* New York: Washington Square Press, 1960.

———. *The Interpretation of Dreams.* New York: Basic Books, 1955.

Frost, Robert. "The Road Not Taken," originally published in *Mountain Interval.* New York: Henry Holt, 1916.

Green, Jay P. *The Interlinear Greek New Testament.* Peabody, Mass.: Hendrickson, 1976.

Gregory, Saint (the Great). *Dialogues*. Translated by Odo John Zimmerman, O.S.B. New York: Fathers of the Church, 1959.

James, William. *The Varieties of Religious Experience*. New York: Longmans, Green & Company, 1925.

Jerome, Saint. *Dogmatic and Polemical Works*. Translated by John N. Hritzu. Washington, D.C.: Catholic University of America Press, 1965.

Jung, C. G. *The Archetypes and the Collective Unconscious*. Part 1, Vol. 9, *Collected Works*. New York: Pantheon-Random House for the Bollingen Foundation, 1959.

———. *Civilization in Transition*. Vol. 10, *Collected Works*. New York: Pantheon-Random House for the Bollingen Foundation, 1964.

———. *The Development of Personality*. Vol. 17, *Collected Works*. New York: Pantheon-Random House for the Bollingen Foundation, 1954.

———. *Freud and Psychoanalysis*. Vol. 4, *Collected Works*. New York: Pantheon-Random House for the Bollingen Foundation, 1961.

———. *Memories, Dreams, Reflections*. Recorded and edited by Aniela Jaffé. New York: Pantheon, 1963.

———. *Mysterium Coniuncionis*. Vol. 14, *Collected Works*. New York: Pantheon-Random House for the Bollingen Foundation, 1963.

———. *The Practice of Psychotherapy*. Vol. 16, *Collected Works*. New York: Pantheon-Random House for the Bollingen Foundation, 1954.

———. *Psychological Types*. London: Routledge & Kegan Paul, 1953.

———. *Psychology and Alchemy*. Vol. 12, *Collected Works*. New York: Pantheon-Random House for the Bollingen Foundation, 1953.

————. *Psychology and Religion: West and East.* Vol. 11, *Collected Works.* New York: Pantheon-Random House for the Bollingen Foundation, 1958.

————. *The Spirit in Man, Art and Literature.* Vol. 15, *Collected Works.* New York: Pantheon-Random House for the Bollingen Foundation, 1944.

————. *The Structure and Dynamics of the Psyche.* Vol. 8, *Collected Works.* New York: Pantheon-Random House for the Bollingen Foundation, 1960.

————. *Symbols of Transformation.* Vol. 5, *Collected Works.* New York: Pantheon-Random House for the Bollingen Foundation, 1956.

————. *Two Essays on Analytical Psychology.* Vol. 7, *Collected Works.* New York: Pantheon-Random House for the Bollingen Foundation, 1953.

Lewis, Lloyd. *Myths after Lincoln.* New York: Grosset & Dunlap, 1957.

Lietzmann, Hans. *A History of the Early Church.* Cleveland, Ohio: World Publishing, 1961.

The Life of the Rev. John Newton. Oradell, N.J.: American Tract Society

MacKenzie, Norman. *Dreams and Dreaming.* London: Aldus Books, 1965.

Miller, Arthur. *After the Fall.* New York: Penguin Books, 1980.

Montague, Ullman, and Nan Zimmerman. *Working with Dreams.* New York: Dell, 1979.

Moustakas, Clark. *Creativity and Conformity.* New York: Van Nostrand Reinhold, 1967.

Ouspensky, P. D. *In Search of the Miraculous.* London: Routledge & Kegan Paul, 1950.

Ratcliff, A. J. *A History of Dreams.* London: Grant Richards, 1923.

Savory, Louis M., Patricia H. Berne, and Strephon Kaplan Williams. *Dreams and Spiritual Growth, A Christian Approach to Dream Work.* New York: Paulist Press, 1984.

A Select Library of the Nicene and Post-Nicene Fathers of the Christian Church. 1st and 2nd series. Grand Rapids, Mich: Eerdmans.

van der Post, Laurens. *The Heart of the Hunter.* New York: William Morrow, 1961.

Van Dusen, Wilson. *The Natural Depth in Man.* New York: Harper & Row, 1972.

Von Grunebaum, E., and Roger Caillois, eds. *The Dream and Human Societies.* Berkeley: University of California Press, 1966.

White, Victor, O. P. *God and the Unconscious.* Cleveland, Ohio: World Publishing, 1961.

Whyte, Lancelot Law. *The Unconscious Before Freud.* New York: Basic Books, 1960.

Wickes, Frances G. *The Inner World of Choice.* New York: Harper & Row, 1963.

Willis, John R., S. J., ed. *The Teachings of the Church Fathers.* New York: Herder & Herder, 1966.

Wolff, Werner. *The Dream: Mirror of Conscience.* New York: Grune & Stratton, 1952.

Woods, Ralph L., ed. *The World of Dreams.* New York: Random House, 1947.

Writings from the Philokalia on Prayer of the Heart. Translated by
E. Kadloubovsky and G. E. H. Palmer. London: Faber & Faber,
1954.

Zolar's Encyclopedia and Dictionary of Dreams. Garden City, N.Y.:
Doubleday, 1963.

Journal Articles

Fisher, Charles. "Psychoanalytic Implications of Recent Research
on Sleep and Dreaming." *Journal of the American Psychoanalytic
Association,* 13, no. 2 (April 1965): 197-303.

Foulkes, W. David. "Dream Reports from Different Stages of Sleep."
Journal of Abnormal and Social Psychology, 65, no. 1 (January
1962): 14-25.

Journal of the Society for Psychical Research 34 (1948).

Morey, Robert. "When Christians Meet Astrology." *The Christian
Herald,* December 1988, 23.

Proceedings. Society for Psychical Research, 10 (1894).

Winson, Jonathan. "The Meaning of Dreams." *Scientific American,*
November 1990, 86-96.